Tresa

Belly Button Blues

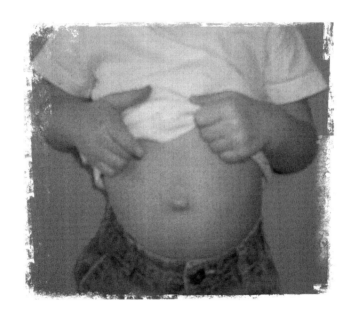

Reflections

Teresa Lee Wendel

The essays in *Belly Button Blues* are related by a precocious nine-year-old with a limited understanding of life and relationships. As an adult, the author has gained insight into the happenings of that summer. *Belly Button Blues*, nonetheless, has stayed true to the imaginings, fears, confusions, and questionings of a child. In her mind, every summer of her life had been the same. For that reason, the time frame of certain reflections may have inaccuracies.

To those who grew up:
Fred, Ted, Ev, Judy,
Mark, Ken, Kathy, and Susie

There is another world,
but it is in this one.

Paul Eluard
1895-1952

Summer, 1962
Everett, Washington
THE JENNINGS ROAD GANG

310 Jennings Road:

Ted and Nancy Cleveland
Teddie, Teresa, Markie, Evie, and Baby Sister Susie

222 Jennings Road:

Frank and Winnie Koenig
Freddie, Judy, Kenny, and Little Kathy

Teresa Lee Cleveland

Belly Button Blues

Contents

Introduction

The mothers on Jennings Road baked cookies, gossiped over the fence, learned how to drive, and occasionally tipped the bottle. We children, their aspiring little hooligans, hijacked tipsy rafts, set fires, jumped off rooftops, broke windows, and ran with pointed sticks.

Because competent adults neither planned nor presided over our outings, we had the swaggering confidence and the run of the neighborhood that was the birthright of our generation.

We engaged in every manner of mischief.

We took life-threatening risks.

We never thought of consequences.

There were no safety nets.

⁓ ⁓

In the junk drawer of every kitchen, there were matchbooks for the taking, and all of us played with fire. Nobody ever got burned—but we almost set our clubhouse ablaze.

We "Tarzaned" across gulches on frayed ropes tied together with granny knots. It would have made for a bit of excitement, but alas, the ropes didn't break.

We rode our bicycles with no hands—one of us balancing on the handlebars, one pedaling, and another bouncing on the rear fender. Markie took a header off the back of Ted's bike and was dizzy for most of a week.

The Silver Lake lifeguards were inattentive, but all of us were exceptional dog paddlers. We seldom came too close to drowning.

We brewed homemade wine using salmonberries, blackberries, huckleberries, blackcaps, thimbleberries, and a package of Fleishman's bread yeast pilfered from a kitchen cupboard. After taking no more than a sip, all of us feared going home smashed.

Teddie leapt into a pile of leaves from an upstairs bedroom window and suffered not so much as a scratch. He subsequently broke his leg bounding off a porch that was two steps high.

We swished from tree to tree and then to the ground on the thin, supple trunks of vine maples that grew in clumps throughout our woodlot. When Markie got stuck near the top of a maple, none of us could coax him to leap for a skinny limb and "parachute" down.

We took turns pumping as high as we could, and then jumped from the swing—attempting to fly. Pinecones marked our landing spots. I was the victor of one round, but pulled my left arm from its socket.

Oh, how I relished the taste of a thick, dry grass stalk—lit on the end and inhaled! Big Betty and Little Betty, cashiers at Midland Gardens, sold us an occasional cigar—no doubt hoping it would make us turn green.

We thumped down the steep stairs in Fred and Judy's house on our bottoms or "sledded" down headfirst on a pillow. No serious injuries were inflicted, but when the pillow ripped, downy feathers floated behind us.

∽ ∾

The Jennings Road kids all grew to adulthood suffering no more than broken bones, black eyes, bumped noggins, and assorted gashes that occasionally needed stitches.

Back then, the world was ours, we owned everything in it, and just about anything could be fixed with a Band-Aid and a thorough cleansing with diluted Lysol disinfectant cleaner.

When You Wish
Upon a Star

"Meteors add more than two million tons of matter to the earth every year," Mr. Werner told his third grade pupils. "That's ten feet deep over the entire earth."

He scanned the classroom and frowned. Nobody was paying attention.

It was the middle of June—two days until summer vacation. I envisioned sleep-outs with the Koenig kids in our backyard—eight mummy bags arranged like spokes on a wheel with all of our heads together.

We'd search for the Seven Sisters.

We'd seek out Venus and Mars.

We'd count each star in the Milky Way.

We'd go mad when the moon was full.

Meteors—those magical falling stars, I dreamily mused as Mr. Werner revealed the secrets of the universe. *Two million tons is a whole lot of wishing!*

All of us would watch for a falling star.

Each child would get a chance for a wish.

I'd wish that our wishes would come true.

∞ ∾

From an early age, I'd believed in magic—the hopeful possibility of miracles, the power to have wishes granted.

Rainbows.

Ringed rocks.

Birthday wishes.

Horseshoes.

Wishbones.

Falling stars.

Beginner's luck.

I put faith in them all. I carried a rabbit's foot in my pocket, crossed my fingers, and searched for four-leaf clovers. I collected lucky pennies. I wished on the first star at dusk.

∞ ∽

Eight pennies jingled in my pocket as I skipped from school to home. I wouldn't waste a single coin on candy before I made a wish. I plunged a hand into my pocket, pulled out a piece of luck, and rubbed it between thumb and finger.

Scanning the roadside, I looked for another penny—one that had landed "heads up" instead of "tails." I was always on the lookout for a charmed potion to make everything better when nothing ever seemed quite right.

Eight lucky pennies weighted down my pocket as I walked the narrow path along the road.

My pockets were heavy with possibilities!

My pockets were filled with power!

Feeling bountiful and bighearted, I tossed a penny onto the pathway to bring good fortune to a down-and-out child—a little girl a lot like me.

Bridge-Dwelling Demons and Booby Traps

My parents discouraged us from mingling with the kids on Olivia Park Road. Their houses were shabbier and more unkempt than ours, and were built on boggy ground. Their road had more potholes. Their ditches were fetid and foul. Broken bicycles and dead car batteries littered their yards. Fences wobbled and fell down.

The dads on Olivia Park Road grunted, snarled, and cussed at their kids. They tossed empty beer bottles into their packed-dirt yards. They shot the bull, chain-smoked, and traded auto parts that were no doubt stolen. Carburetors, gas tanks, passenger seats, and radiators sailed every which-way as they tore apart the family car.

The moms were seldom about.

∞ ∽

Our rough-and-tumble rivals to the north—the kids from Olivia Park—had staked a claim on the tangled and untrailed Nether Woods that divided our two roads. A spectacular pond sat rank and languid within its midst. Oh, how we coveted those murky waters and the tipsy raft beached on its shore! Some years before, an industrious lad had chopped down a stand of alder saplings and then lashed them together with twine. The raft was grand enough to convey three kids.

On sultry days when our rivals seemed sluggish, we ventured into their hostile hinterland to gaze upon the pond. We pranced along the muddy shoreline. We rolled up our pant legs and waded in the tepid shallows.

Sometimes we even dared to launch the raft.

෨ ൞

The day was sultry.

Our rivals seemed sluggish.

We sallied forth to their pond.

Scratched by brambles and mosquito-bit, our ragged band formed a line along the bank. My bare feet sank into the mud as I scanned the algae-green water for flashes of orange within its depths.

"I bet some kid dumped those goldfish in the pond when we were babies," Freddie said, pointing out a school.

After adapting to the scummy water, the goldfish had grown five times larger than normal and had multiplied their numbers. Some of them were twelve inches long! Utilizing nets and homemade poles, we'd often made attempts to catch one. Not one of us had ever succeeded.

But, not to be deterred, Fred, Teddie, Markie, and Ken boarded the raft. I gave it a push into deeper water. Freddie, the oldest, claimed his role as captain. He had in mind a good fishing spot, but nobody followed his orders. All four boys jabbed their sturdy poles into the muddy bottom with their own destinations in mind.

Having been left high and dry on the shore, we girls waded up to our knees and then plunked our lines into the water. The goldfish weren't biting. The mosquitoes were. They filled their bellies with our blood.

Suddenly, Teddie jerked on his pole, let out a holler, and pulled in his line.

Evie and Judy screamed.

I dropped my fishing net.

My big brother had snagged a catfish!

Four excited anglers did a little dance. The tipsy raft wobbled—and into the water they fell.

We brought the hapless fish home in a bait bucket where it lived in the bottom of a galvanized washtub until it died—most likely of starvation.

∽ ⌒

My playmates and I looked forward to pet funerals with morbid delight. Whether it was a mouse the cat had maimed, an arthritic but beloved pooch, or a relocated catfish from The Nether Woods, anything that came up dead was laid to rest beneath a crooked tree in the woodlot behind our houses on the south side of Jennings Road. If dead pets were scarce, even a belly-up beetle might be given a burial.

We entombed the catfish in a shoebox, dug a hole deep enough for a school of fish, lowered the box into the grave, and then covered it over with dirt. Judy, Evie,

Little Kathy, and I scattered flowers that we'd pilfered from a neighbor's yard. Because Freddie was Catholic, he concluded the rite with a prayer.

∽ ∾

"That poor fish will be much happier swimming in a golden pond in heaven," my Sunday School teacher said when I told her about its demise and subsequent burial on the following Sabbath.

According to my Bible teacher, angel children were not issued rafts and fishing poles upon admittance through The Pearly Gates. That revelation caused me to desire nothing more than an earthly life. I was not inclined to trade my fishing pole for a halo and angel wings even if the streets in heaven were paved with gold.

The sweetly smiling Sunday School ladies took perverse delight in frightening their students with tales about remorseless sinners who were given a taste of damnation as they lingered on their deathbeds.

"Beneath them, maggots are spread out as a couch," my teacher claimed, "and worms are their covering."

Although still very much alive, slowly, ever so slowly, the wrongdoer descended into hell. First his toes got hot. Then his legs burned up. Within minutes, he was up to his belly. Writhing upon his bed, the sinner pleaded and begged for mercy while his distraught wife and wide-eyed children looked on. But it was too late. He sank into the fire and brimstone—one dying breath at a time.

"The fear of the Lord prolongeth thy days," my teacher said, "but the years of the wicked shalt be shortened."

The Sunday School teacher further informed me that my fate had been determined on the very day that I'd been born. No matter how good I tried to be, if God had assigned me to hell on the day of my birth, I was going to hell. Because there was no sense in even trying, I resigned myself to The Lava Pit.

It's no wonder that we were abnormally intrigued by the afterlife. Other children, I was told, strived to reach China when they embarked on a digging project. But our gang, outfitted with picks and shovels, hoped to encounter Satan himself. The holes that riddled our woodlot grew wide and deep, but we never reached The Depths of Despair. Dirty and disheartened, we salvaged a 2x8 from a lumber pile behind someone's garage and placed it over the hole so we had a bridge to bounce across.

But ravenous trolls weren't offered shelter beneath our rickety bridges.

"The Devil lives under here," we told the pesky siblings amongst us, Kenny, Markie, and Little Kathy.

While they sought out a cheerier play spot—a lofty perch in a maple tree or a prickly pathway through the salmonberries—we older ones excavated another pit. Upon completion of the dig, we combed backyards for dog poop, mixed up buckets of mud, and cut armloads of sticker bushes to line the pit's bottom. Tree branches, fern fronds, and moss camouflaged its nasty contents.

Riddled with booby traps, inhabited by bridge-dwelling demons, and defended by wily waifs wielding sharp-pointed sticks, our shimmering and wondrous woodlot held many dangers for simpering siblings, wayfaring wanderers, and nosy parents alike.

Armed and eager for battle, we rolled up our shirtsleeves and pant legs.

We painted our faces with mud.

We whooped and hollered and howled.

And then, we waited.

And waited.

And waited.

When even the rough-and-tumble bunch from Olivia Park Road failed to invade our domain, we were obliged to lure the young innocents, Kenny, Markie, and Little Kathy, toward our traps instead.

Skeleton Key in the Closet

We tilted back our heads and looked up at the dormer window. If only we could squirm through that portal! We'd find cobwebs, mouse droppings, and inexplicable phenomena—a silver candelabra with yellowed candles mysteriously lit, a ladder that broke through the roof and reached to the stars, specters, spooks, and spirits eager to waylay us, creaky doors too numerous to count, and a mazy passage leading to a chamber of wondrous horrors.

Great-Auntie Virgie stood on the porch beneath that attic window and beckoned us inside.

Our aunt and uncle's house had not been furnished with rambunctious children in mind. Spindly antique tables displayed fragile and costly ornaments. A dainty sofa and matching chairs would surely collapse if you plopped upon them. There were wobbly lamps with stained glass shades, and mirrors on every wall. Even the kitchen cupboards, filled with fine china, had been fitted with glass-paned doors.

But fragile furnishings went unheeded when we visited Auntie Virgie and Uncle Bill. A ruthless rooting of their house ensued the moment we stepped inside. Hunting for the key to their attic had been our pastime for many years.

So while Auntie doted on Baby Sister Susie and Mom enjoyed the fleeting reprieve, my siblings and I bent purposefully to the task at hand. Bric-a-brac was upturned and repositioned, and then upturned a second time. One child snooped through a bedroom closet while another slid under the bed. Arms were thrust beneath cushions of the couch. Book pages were riffled. Cupboards were probed. Markie distracted Mom while Teddie ransacked a drawer. Evie poked a finger into a furnace vent.

"You kids still haven't figured out where Virgie's hidden that key?" Uncle Bill inquired as we rummaged through his study.

"Can't you just give us a hint?" I besought.

But alas, Uncle Bill's lips were sealed. Despite our tireless commitment, the elusive key remained at-large. Yet, never despairing, I still hoped someday to breach the attic stronghold so I could probe the mysteries within it.

Auntie Virgie passed by the doorway and grinned. "Any of you up to a game of cards?"

We trailed after her to the breakfast nook where she thumbed playing cards off the deck for a rollicking game of Go Fish. Arranging the cards for Concentration, Auntie helped us find the matches. Not one of us could beat her at Slap Jack or Crazy Eights.

Although she excelled at children's card games, Auntie Virgie was a serious gambler too. Poker was her game of choice. At their Friday night card parties, Uncle Bill served up whiskey in tiny shot glasses. Cigar smoke fogged the room. It was rumored that my aunt kept a loaded gun beneath her apron to keep the players in line.

Oh, how I loved my spirited auntie! I couldn't wait to grow up so I could knock down shots of whiskey, smoke cigars, and try my hand at Poker. When that day arrived, Auntie would deal me a winning hand. And then, in lieu of the million dollars that she'd be bound to pay me when she lost the game, I'd demand the key to her attic instead.

Group Therapy

The loquacious mothers on Jennings Road called themselves The Waggin' Tongues. Their neighborhood social club was not made up of civic-minded do-gooders who organized food drives for the needy, delivered soup to the sickly, or knitted hats and mittens for the homeless. The singular purpose of its members was to wag their tongues.

Although they lived outside the bounds of our neighborhood, a number of women had infiltrated the club by way of friendships that went back to childhood, husbands who worked together at the paper mill, or attendance at the same church. But whether the mom lived on Jennings Road, Emander, or Colleen Drive, the close-knit group looked out for each other—and for each other's children besides.

Every Wednesday evening, the neighborhood ladies joined company at a different home. The hostess' only obligation to her guests was to offer them cocktails, coffee, and a sinful dessert. Butter-stained and sauce-splattered Betty Crocker cookbooks provided recipes for such treats, yet the holders of those "old family recipes passed down for generations" had been sworn to secrecy.

During the course of their neighborly gatherings, every manner of complaint and hardship was aired. Inattentive husbands, misbehaving children, meddlesome in-laws, money woes, and the latest weight-loss diet were discussed, analyzed, bemoaned, and tossed about. Embellishing their grievances with exaggerations and outright lies, each woman attempted to trump the others, or to make a better point.

To be absent or to arrive tardy at these soirees left the missing Waggin' Tongue, her husband, her in-laws, her children, and even her dog up for dissection.

Attendance was one hundred percent.

∽ ∾

It was Mom's night to entertain. TV trays had been set out in the living room. A pot of coffee perked on the stove. Dessert plates, cups and saucers, a cream and sugar set, eating utensils, and white linen napkins were lined up on the kitchen counter. A fabulously lopsided three-layer cake commanded center stage atop the table.

Mom untied her gingham apron and surveyed the house. Walking briskly into the bathroom, she fluffed her hair, pinched her cheeks, and then applied lipstick before the mirror. I loved it when Mom "dolled herself up," as Dad would say. She looked like a Hollywood starlet.

As the neighbor ladies tapped up the walk wearing high heels, hats, and clingy dresses, four wide-awake children were ushered off to bed and out of sight. In spite of whispered threats from Mom, Evie and I descended the stairs to eavesdrop in the shadowy hallway.

The cloying scent of Evening in Paris wafted into our peeking place. The cobalt blue cologne bottle could be found atop the bedroom dresser of every lady on Jennings Road. My sister and I scooted on our bottoms toward the doorway. We eyed the tittering women as they forked down mouthfuls of cake that oozed with buttercream frosting.

Mom's delectable, cock-eyed cakes were renowned on Jennings Road. Five hundred toothpicks were all that held them together. Fifty pounds of frosting kept the layers from crumbling apart. Never could she flop the round layers out of the pans without cracking them in half. Nary a woman faulted her for such failures, but Mom's inability to construct an upright three-layer cake caused her endless angst.

"Your cakes aren't much to look at, Nancy," Winnie remarked, licking her fingers, "but the flavor can't be beat."

"I'd give up a front tooth for the recipe," another said.

Mom raised an eyebrow and smiled.

Despite much pressure from fellow club members, she declined to divulge the secret ingredient in her cakes—salty tears of frustration that added even more moisture to the luscious batter.

Clutching stomachs that growled for want of cake and gooey icing, Evie and I sat cross-legged in the hallway. The living room walls vibrated with chatter. The neighbors argued, agreed, interrupted each other, and then argued and agreed anew. Voices rose and fell.

Laughter broke out. The ladies' drinks were freshened up.

Evie leaned her head upon my shoulder. I rested mine against hers. The muted murmur of women's voices was more soothing than a lullaby. When snatches of conversation floated into the hallway, the dreamy phrases blurred into a strange and obscure tongue. It was a language, I imagined, that only a mother could master. The unintelligible words, if I could translate them, would clarify the bewildering secrets that governed social interactions and other mysteries that perplexed a child like me.

I nudged my sister who was on the verge of nodding off. After downing two rounds of strong drink, the ladies soon would be standing in line for the loo. Lest we be discovered, Evie and I crept back up the stairs.

Before I settled into bed and gently drifted off, I sent forth a fervent prayer.

If You love me like the church ladies tell me, please don't let the cake platter be empty when I wake up tomorrow morning.

Inspiration in a Lumber Pile

Kenny and Markie
building a hut in the woodlot

Nobody knew where they came from.

Nobody knew how they got there.

Not even the owner of the home could apprise you of their source.

The lumber, no doubt, had been salvaged from building sites, remodeling projects, and demolitions in far-flung and unknown places. It came in odd lengths, assorted widths, and varied grades. The boards had been heaved into stacks willy-nilly. Protruding nails pointed every which-way—all of them rusty and bent.

Such heaps of lumber could be found behind every garage on Jennings Road.

∽ ∾

The aspiring young carpenters amongst us pawed and picked through the scrap piles on a quest for building materials. We rooted and rearranged. Without fail, one of us would drive a nail through the sole of a rubber flip-flop and into a foot. After wrapping an arm around the necks of two buddies, the howling victim would be hastened home between them straightaway.

With so many hazards in our own backyards, the neighborhood mothers had good reason to regale us with gruesome tales of luckless victims of lockjaw—hale and hearty men struck down by a rusty, bent nail.

A locked jaw? We clenched and gritted our teeth.

None of us was sure of the symptoms, but the name alone gave cause for alarm.

Lockjaw. We speculated as to what that might mean.

"You couldn't eat," Freddie said.

"Then you'd starve to death?" That was Markie.

"You couldn't breathe either," Ted said, giving no heed to our brother's alarm.

"Yeah, you could." I placed an arm across Markie's back and gave his shoulder a squeeze. "You know— through your nose?"

"Not if it was plugged up with snot."

If the victim was current on his tetanus shot—and, given our record, most of us were current—he would still be obliged to spend the rest of the day with his foot soaking in a half-filled bucket of diluted Lysol. That common household disinfectant was not only the preferred product for cleaning toilets and scrubbing kitchen linoleum, it was employed by the mothers on Jennings Road to disinfect punctures, scratches, scrapes, cuts, mosquito bites, and bee stings besides. Our mothers, backwoods country doctors, had agreed that four hours of soaking was the minimum time required to accomplish a cure—four hours of sitting on the porch steps with your foot in a bucket while bursts of laughter, the pounding of hammers, and the rhythmic rasp of handsaws resounded in the woods beyond.

∾ ∾

When we weren't soaking a foot in a bucket of Lysol, we busied ourselves hammering forts and tree houses together. Our hideouts were fantastic feats of architecture with windows that shuttered closed, creaky trapdoors, and rooftop balconies with incredible views. Markie and Kenny, although small, seemed particularly adept at tree house building. Their wondrous creations perched on every limb that might hold them in the woods behind our houses. The shelters were often so small, they had to scrunch up to fit inside.

As fine as those tree houses were, they were nowhere near as marvelous as the downhill racers that Fred and Teddie designed. In an ongoing search for suitable wheels for their go-carts, they rummaged through garden sheds and garages up and down Jennings Road.

An ancient baby pram—of the style that nannies pushed in England—had been left to molder in a corner of the Koenig's garage. Fred and Teddie coveted its wheels. Not only did they have ball bearings, they were attached to axles besides. Never before had the boys scored such a prize.

After chancing upon that find, Freddie made the mistake of asking permission before disassembling the artifact and making off with its precious plunder. Pitiful pleas and promises to do extra chores did not sway Freddie's father, Frank. His request was summarily denied.

Not to be dissuaded, Fred and Teddie sallied forth on a salvaging expedition to the county dump. Their search yielded nary a similar set of wheels. Resourceful lads that they were, however, the engineers improvised. They gleaned the wheels of disabled lawnmowers that had been abandoned in sundry backyards—without first asking permission, of course.

The body of the go-cart was a 2x12 length of lumber. A 2x4, long enough to protrude six to eight inches off each side, was hammered on crosswise at one end of the body. It served as the rear axle. To facilitate steering, another 2x4 was bolted to the front of the cart. If a bolt couldn't be had, a sturdy nail, pounded in and then bent over, would suffice. Because the wheels weren't mounted on axles, they were attached to each end of the crosspieces with long nails. A backrest was hammered onto the body of the cart at an angle, and held in place with a prop. Enough room remained behind it to carry a kneeling passenger who clung to the seat for his life.

The carts were steered by pulling on ropes fastened to each side of the front crossbar, but also could be maneuvered by moving the crossbar with your feet. Short lengths of 2x2s nailed to each side at the rear of the cart could be scraped on the asphalt to slow down the machine. The brakes were seldom employed. We strove for optimum speed and maximum distance as we sped out-of-control down the Jennings Road hill over potholes, loose gravel, and asphalt patches.

The neighborhood handyman, Leo, lived in a shack beyond the hill near the end of Jennings Road. After a bus ride into town, his companion, Fat Hazel, hobbled toward the hill leaning on a long pole. Kindhearted Fred and Teddie offered her a free ride home on the back of one of their carts. In spite of knees that creaked and aching hips, Hazel graciously, and quite wisely, declined.

The Outer Limits

Mom and Dad
at the Lord's Hill Ranch

I awoke in the gloom of night and sat up in bed.
Something didn't feel right.

Something didn't look right.

Something didn't sound right.

Something was wrong.

Within a few frightening moments, however, the mystery was solved. I was spending the night with Grandpa Cleve and Grandma Mable! My sister Evie slumbered at my side.

My grandparents lived on a ranch near the top of Lord's Hill in Snohomish—a ranch that housed nary a horse, cow, pig, chicken, or duck. The barn was empty. So was the pigsty. The chicken coop had been abandoned as well. Another structure of unknown usage had collapsed in upon itself. Blackberry vines engulfed its rubble. Only one building on those many acres—aside from the house—had a purpose, and I sorely needed to make use of it as soon as I worked up the courage.

Oh, if only I had been plumbed like my brothers who were privileged to pee out the back door!

A nudge to Evie's shoulder didn't cause her to stir, so I poked her a second time even harder. My sister switched thumbs and continued to suck. So, flustered and afraid, I crept alone through the house so as not to rouse Gram and Grandpa, yet hoping with all my heart that I would—but I didn't. With a hard turn of the knob, the back door creaked open. I stepped into the moist gloom of midnight. Shivering on the stoop, I beheld my destination from afar. The sorry structure perched atop a rise some distance from the house.

Barefoot and unbrave, I picked my way up the path to the lowly outhouse. Strange and indescribable creatures had been spawned, so I believed, in the primordial mire of its dungy depths. I anticipated a fierce and bloody battle with hordes of loathsome, smelly creatures as they swarmed forth from the odious pit as soon as I trespassed on their realm.

I pulled up my nightgown, plopped upon the throne, and peed as fast as I could. The ghoulish creature with clutching fingers who sought to entrap me in its putrid pit was lumbering and clumsy and very unfleet of foot. Before it scaled the sides of the heinous hole and grabbed my bottom, I hopped off the seat, thrust open the door, and fled on nimble feet to the house.

I settled into bed beside my sister who still noisily sucked on her thumb. Since no one else was awake to do it, I congratulated myself for avoiding capture by grisly creatures of the night. The escapade did not leave me entirely unscathed, however. On my sprint back to the house, I'd treaded upon dozens of slimy and insidious slugs—the only creatures that multiplied and thrived on Grandpa Cleve and Grandma Mable's ranch.

Holy Rollers

"Jesus Christ!"
"What in heaven's name?"
"God damn it!"
"To hell with you!"

Such expressions—followed by upraised voices and the slamming of doors—occasionally assailed the eardrums of the young innocents on Jennings Road. Such expressions were my first introduction to divine rulers and their realms in the heavens above and the earth below.

∽ ∾

My parents were not God-fearing. They had little regard for religion, in fact. But when the newly-constructed Open Bible Sunday School had opened its portals some years before, my siblings and I mingled amongst its devotees.

On Sunday mornings, Mom pressed a nickel into each of our palms for the collection plate, and then scooted us out the door and on our way. Teddie, Ev, Markie, and I trudged a mile to the church, squirmed in our chairs for two hours of instruction, and then tramped the mile home. For a mere twenty cents, my folks got a three-hour respite from their energetic, hell-raising rascals.

∽ ⌒

Dressed in our Sunday-best hand-me-downs, the four of us siblings waded the drainage ditches on our way to church. We sought out valuable treasures hidden in the lanky grass and algae slime—empty beer bottles that could be cashed in at Midland Gardens, the neighborhood grocery store, for a penny deposit.

Arms laden with brown bottles, we arrived for our Sunday School classes with sodden hemlines and pant legs, mucky shoes, soiled socks, and grubby hands. We lined up our booty inside the vestibule.

∽ ⌒

I loved the sincere but misguided Sunday School ladies with their stiff, weeklong hairdos who gave us instruction every Sabbath while Mom and Dad lounged in bed. I wanted to feel their conviction, yet I was reluctant to put faith in a frivolous Father who might grant me everlasting life in heaven, or condemn me to an eternity in hell.

"You mean no matter how good I am, God already knows if I go Up or Down when I die?"

The teacher steepled her fingers beneath her chin, and then grimly nodded her head. "He knoweth your beginning. He knoweth your end."

Her blind acceptance of such a doctrine and the futility of it all made me cry. Hell and damnation, I was certain, would be my lot.

"No use in blubbering," the teacher said, swiping at my tears with a tissue, "God won't change his mind."

∾ ∾

I craned forward in my seat as my teacher chronicled the legend of Gideon's fleece.

"If God wet down the fleece during the night and everything else around it stayed dry," she said, "it would be a sign to Gideon that the Almighty was on his side."

A test! How simple! I smiled.

Like Gideon, I needed assurance that God held me dear. Straightaway, a plan came to mind.

Because I lacked a fleece, I used my sweater instead. I placed it in a corner of our attic bedroom, opened my Holy Bible, and read the passage in Judges aloud.

Behold, I will put a fleece of wool in the floor; and if the dew be on the fleece only, and it be dry upon all the earth beside, then shall I know that thou wilt save Israel by mine hand, as thou hast said.

And it was so: for he rose up early on the morrow, and thrust the fleece together, and wringed the dew out of the fleece, a bowl full of water.

I slept in fits and starts that night, excited. I rose up early on the morrow, but alas, when I thrust my sweater together, it be dry. Nary a drop of water filled my bowl.

Because my Bible teacher encouraged forgiveness, I granted the Almighty justification for His failure to give notice to me.

Maybe God was occupied last night with a needier child,
I thought.

I gave Him a second chance, a third, a fourth, and a desperate fifth. Yet, upon rising up early on the morrow of each of five days, my sweater be dry once again.

For all of five nights, I never gave up on God, but for a certainty, He'd forgotten me.

∞ ∞

I envied the pious parishioners who would cry out *Amen! Praise Jesus! Hallelujah!* every time the minister took a breath between his abysmal cries of fire and brimstone. I wanted to raise my arms heavenward and cry *Yes, Lord Jesus!*—all the while hoping that God would heed my entreaty and forget, perhaps, that He'd consigned me to hell on the day of my birth.

But I never raised my arms toward heaven. I was too self-conscious to holler out in church besides. Despite my desire to be devout, I couldn't conjure up affection for the capricious God introduced at The Open Bible Sunday School. I straggled home when the service ended—arms full of beer bottles, my dress a mess, and my braids undone.

"Lord Almighty! Would you look at you?" my mom would sigh by way of a prayer.

Sixty Minutes

Teddie, Teresa, Evie, and Markie
at Silver Lake

"No swimming for an hour after you eat that sandwich." Mom filled a Mason jar with ice cubes and Kool-Aid, and then tightened down the lid. "Sixty minutes—you hear me? And not a second less!"

My playmates and I took exception to anything our mothers might tell us as soon as we were out of their range. All of us, however, obeyed the sixty-minute rule to the second. Not a child amongst us wished to sink like a rock to the muddy bottom of Silver Lake—a fate known to befall children who so much as stuck a toe in the water before an hour had elapsed after eating their lunches.

It seemed like drowning was the only danger that troubled the mothers on Jennings Road. Strangers lurking along our route to the lake did not concern them. We traversed a busy byway with a narrow shoulder, but traffic advisories were never aired. Our mothers entrusted their offspring, besides, to lifeguards who chatted with their girlfriends and buddies instead of maintaining watch over their dog-paddling charges.

"You'll get a cramp and that'll be the end of you," Mom reminded before blithely sending us on our way.

Dragging raggedy towels and carrying jam sandwiches in a grocery sack, we joined up with the Koenig kids, and then trudged two miles to the lake.

We ate our lunch at a picnic table in the midst of a dried-up field within the bounds of the park. The table's weathered boards had been carved up with the initials of every child who had ever dog-paddled in Silver Lake.

Mindful of the required sixty minutes, we took turns checking the clock at the concession stand. Oh, how we craved the scrumptious treats beyond its counter! Our mothers generously had provided the ten cents per patron required to enter the park, so we dared not plead for nickels to purchase Popsicles, popcorn, or chocolate bars besides.

"What? Do you think I'm made of money?" Mom likely would have asked. "Money doesn't grow on trees, you know."

∽ ℘

"If there was a way to sneak in…" Freddie had said as we trooped down Stockshow Road on our way to the lake that day.

"We could spend our dimes on candy!" the rest of us shouted.

But alas, a scouting expedition along the perimeter of the fence revealed neither loose boards nor a spot to burrow. We sought out an alternate route.

"We could swim under the dock," Evie said.

"If we could hold our breath that long," That was Judy.

"I've seen the big kids do it," I said.

"But what if someone catches us?" Markie didn't like to get his face wet. He was wary of the water besides.

"Mom'll kill us if she finds out." That prospect unnerved Kenny.

Both boys were too little and too scared to be implicated in a break-in. So were the rest of us, but we still blamed our kid brothers for the foiled attempt.

∞ ∞

After slathering each other's backs with Johnson's baby oil spiked with iodine, the eight of us spread our towels side-by-side to stake our claim on the beach. We soaked up the white-hot sun for the rest of the hour. It didn't matter if our skin burned until it blistered. Within a week, we'd be engaged with the delightful task of peeling the dead skin off each other's backs. On such occasions, we competed to see who could strip off the biggest piece of skin.

Our neighbor Nicky proved to be the favored burn victim. After his mom and dad had divorced, Mrs. Ross moved into the rental next door while her ex-husband kept possession of the family home and swimming pool. Because Mr. Ross employed a housekeeper, we believed he was a billionaire—or at least he had a money tree. All of us envied Nicky and his sister Diana who stayed weekends with their indulgent dad.

"We swim in the pool all day and eat ice cream and popcorn for dinner every night," Nicky bragged.

On Monday morning, he returned to the Jennings Road rental looking much like a boiled crab. Before he left again on Friday night, the skin of his entire back could be pulled off in a single, wet sheet. We drew straws to determine who got the pleasure to peel it.

∽ ⌒

Once the hour allotted by our mothers had elapsed, we leapt from our towels and bolted for the dock. Its warped boards burned our feet. A wooden float bobbed twenty-five yards beyond the dock—across the perilous, winking waters of Silver Lake. Two diving boards and a tall platform had been installed on that favored haven of the older kids. We aimed to own that float.

Whether by dog-paddling solo or clinging to the back of an older sibling or pal, we cannonballed off the dock and made our way toward the rapturous, oversized raft. Oblivious to our gurgling and thrashing, the lifeguards traded puffs on a cigarette while ogling the baby-oiled girls sprawled on beach towels before the lifeguard station. Gasping, sputtering, and choking on mouthfuls of water, we heaved ourselves onto the float. It never occurred to any of us that we might drown. We had waited sixty minutes after eating our sandwiches, after all.

∽ ⌒

A girl my age—someone's sister, cousin, or neighbor—came up missing some hours later. The lifeguards cleared the swimming area for a search. Although we lingered on the shoreline for quite some time, the girl hadn't been pulled from the water before we were obliged to tromp home.

We never found out whether the missing child simply had wandered back to her house without telling her companions, or if she'd washed up on the beach later that day—lifeless, pale, fish-nibbled, and bloated.

We concluded it was the latter, of course.

If only she'd waited sixty minutes after eating, we agreed, and then all of us shook our heads.

Gypsy Blood

My grandma Mable threatened to sell me to the gypsies whenever I misbehaved. The delightful prospect of traveling around the world in a colorful wagon caused me to test Gram's limits often in an effort to achieve that reward. Ever hopeful that gypsies might be encamped in a nearby glen, my heart would thump within my chest—quickening with expectation.

Gypsies!
Rovers, ramblers, rolling stones!
Travelers, tinkers, tramps!
Wandering wildlings!
Desultory drifters!
Nomads of a noble class…

Oh, to be counted amongst such untamed mortals! The very mention of them made me dizzy.

I imagined starry nights, campfires, a gold tooth, bare feet, and no more school. I would paint my wagon with curlicues and twining flowers. I would braid my horse's mane, and tie silk ribbons to its tail. The lines on a palm, the draw of a card, and the mist within a crystal ball would reveal their frightful secrets to me.

The gypsy maiden!
Eyes outlined with kohl.
Lips reddened with the juice of a berry.
Long hair seductively tangled.

Slender fingers bejeweled with rings.

A swirling skirt of silk.

A bewitching peasant blouse.

A gold nose ring—and ear bobs too.

I'll be the most sought after girl in the land!

So whenever I took a break from misbehaving, I threaded tiny bells onto a shoelace, tied it around an ankle, and danced in circles as I awaited the appearance of my swarthy gypsy lord.

He was sure to arrive any day.

Ashes to Ashtrays

Once a month, my auntie Sis received boxes of Welfare commodities from the U.S. government. The free food fascinated and enthralled me.

Oatmeal, flour, sugar, and cornmeal came packaged in five-pound portions—their contents stamped in bold, black letters across the brown bags. There were jars of peanut butter with generic labels, and blocks of processed cheese. Weevils were often discovered in the cornmeal bags. Grubs wormed through the oatmeal and flour. Auntie's unusual dinners featured processed cheese, shortening, powdered milk, raisins, rice, and the occasional crunchy weevil and grub that her hazel eyes had failed to find.

When Auntie accepted a job as a letter carrier for the United States Postal Service, I was stunned.

With all that free cheese and peanut butter for the asking, I thought, *why would Auntie even want to work?*

She was a determined woman, however, and with her earnings bought a second-hand car.

∽ ∾

"You kids get down from there before you break your necks," Auntie Sis hollered out the kitchen window.

Toni and I were perched on the roof of her garage.

My cousins lived on a street lined with cement sidewalks instead of ditches. Their garage was entered by way of an alley rather than a graveled drive.

Walkways!

Alleys!

So urbane and civilized!

Yet as much as I admired their "city limits" lifestyle replete with streets, avenues, and boulevards bounded by sidewalks and alleys, I pitied my cousins even more for their want of a woodlot, ponds, swamps, and streams behind their house.

Auntie stepped onto her back porch. "You two be careful now. My best friend in second grade broke every bone in her body when she fell off a roof," she hollered.

Auntie's hair-raising remembrances always featured hapless children who'd been maimed, mauled, or murdered in unlikely and frightening ways.

"You'll go blind if you stare at the sun like that, Treesie," she yelled up to me.

I scrunched my eyes and squinted into the sunlight anyhow, searching for celestial bodies. I wanted to be the first woman to live on Mars, faraway and lonely. I wanted to see the rings that circled Saturn like giant hula-hoops. I wanted to fly to Venus, a shimmering planet, second in distance from the sun. It was named after a beautiful goddess—a powerful woman like I hoped to be.

"Get off that roof this minute, you hear me?"

Toni and I eased our bottoms down the slope. We dropped from the eaves and followed her into the kitchen, banging the screen door behind us. Auntie took a soulful drag on her cigarette, tilted back her head, blew out the smoke, and then stubbed out the cigarette in an ashtray. When I counted eleven butts, a grim and grisly vision of blackened lungs came to mind.

Auntie never had told us not to smoke. She had replaced that lecture with a far-fetched tale featuring a young lad whose body was grotesquely charred when he was playing with matches.

My aunt tousled the tops of our heads. Toni and I fastened our arms about her waist, and then buried our faces in her soft belly.

Oh, how I idolized my energetic auntie who laughed and hollered and hugged her kids. She spent her money on bags of burgers, and toys that fell apart too soon. My little cousins lived in pleasant confusion—their house in glorious disarray. Two laundry baskets spilled over with dirty clothes, but Auntie gave no notice. When she got around to the washing, play pants and tee shirts seldom found their way to rickety dressers with their drawers yawning half open. If a clean glass wasn't at hand, we drank straight from the faucet. Auntie seldom got riled when we raced through the house—bouncing on the furniture, sliding down the stairs, skidding across the linoleum, and jumping out the windows.

The radio blared as she struck a match to light another cigarette. She hummed the tune to a dreamy love song, but her life was hardly romantic. The only man Auntie had ever loved was no account, no good, and nowhere near parole. Uncle Eddie, an unreformable felon, got out of prison only long enough to give her another baby. Shortly after the pregnancy was confirmed, the long arm of the law snatched him up and threw him in the slammer again.

Yes, Auntie's life was a mess indeed.

I wanted to grow up to be just like her.

The Great Unknowns

The aspiring sleuths on Jennings Road quietly nosed about the neighborhood, pausing at times to climb a tree or to burrow within a hedge—the better to spy on unwitting neighbors. We crouched behind sofas or outside a door to eavesdrop on adult conversations that left us unsettled and perplexed. Husbands were compared, mother-in-laws berated, and monthly periods or the lateness of them—whatever they might be—were discussed at length. Some of the mothers suggested faking a headache at bedtime. For what reason? I couldn't guess. If that didn't work, they could fake a period. The use of condoms—or the non-use of them—was a well-worn topic. Condoms were some sort of accessory—like a hatpin or a belt—I surmised.

When other kids were playing "doctor," we opted to train as private eyes. Our little gang patrolled Jennings Road toting flashlights, baseball bats, and cap guns. All of us had ordered cheap walkie-talkies from an ad placed in the back pages of a comic book. We gleaned magnifying glasses from Cracker Jack boxes, and then sought out fingerprints. The previous Christmas, toy handcuffs had been given to the more fortunate amongst us—not me. When we failed to find bad guys to cuff, we apprehended Kenny, Markie, and Little Kathy instead, and secured them to a tree. The young tagalongs were always obliging, and surrendered without a fight. Often we forgot to free them.

We spent more time rummaging through rubbish cans looking for incriminating clues than was healthy for normal children. We snooped through medicine cabinets and dresser drawers. Weighty, top-secret messages were relayed in an obscure tongue, Pig Latin, that my mother graciously had taught us. All of us quickly became bilingual.

"I can make invisible ink out of lemon juice," Freddie bragged.

To our astonishment, it worked. To read such messages, we procured matches and then passed the flame beneath the paper. As the paper warmed, a top-secret message appeared. Most of Freddie's memos, however, went up in flames before we got a chance to read them.

∽ ∾

Oh, how we longed to probe the mysteries of The Bee Man's life!

Only Leo claimed ever to have met him. Although our neighborhood handyman was given to drunken tall tales and out-and-out lies, not even the grownups disbelieved him. Leo was curiously vague, however, in regards to The Bee Man on the day of our interrogation. When we plied him for details about the recluse at the end of the road, Leo disappeared into his moss-covered hovel and returned with a jar of honey.

"Got this from The Bee Man before any of you was even born. This here's the last of a dozen jars."

Because Freddie was the tallest and least likely to drop it, Leo passed the jar to him. Squinting his eyes, Fred examined it intently—scanning for fingerprints, no doubt. The rest of us pressed in upon him to behold the jar at closer range.

On account of the bees that might swarm about us and sting on command, that jar of golden honey was as close as we got to The Bee Man that day.

∽ ∾

BLIND WOMAN WITHIN!!!! announced a sign tacked to the front door of a squat little house halfway down the Jennings Road hill. A large, dusty window at the front of the house was neither draped nor covered by a shade. The lamp before it glowed cheerily day and night.

Hoping to catch a glimpse of our elusive neighbor, all eight of us children lounged beneath the cooling boughs of two massive maple trees in her front yard. Eyes fixed on the window before us, we awaited her appearance. Although we passed many afternoons at our stakeout, The Blind Woman Within stayed out of sight.

Yet if we so much as blinked an eye or turned a head, we could expect that a tray holding a plate of cookies, a pitcher of Kool-Aid, and eight drinking glasses would materialize before the closed side door. Because the refreshments hadn't popped up through the porch boards, we wondered how The Blind Woman Within had accomplished such a feat unnoticed by eight detectives.

"She's blind *and* invisible," I suggested as we filled our glasses with Kool-Aid.

Because there was no other explanation, seven heads nodded in accord.

As much as we desired to behold The Blind Woman Within and to ply her with questions, we knocked upon her door but once a year—on Halloween night. Not only did we hope to be rewarded with a look at her face, we also strove to trick or treat The Blind Woman Within before her supply of candy ran out. She was the only neighbor who doled out nickel candy bars rather than the usual wax paper-wrapped homemade cookies and popcorn balls, or beggarly penny candies. In a brimming basket before her side door, the candy bars were ours for the taking.

On Halloween night the previous fall, the girls amongst our group favored gypsy or witch's garb while the boys masqueraded as hobos or Indian chiefs. We disdained those children who donned store-bought costumes and unimaginative masks, or those disguised as mundane, common ghosts. Our makeshift and quirky costumes we'd proudly designed ourselves. Grownups played no part in a holiday made exclusively for kids.

Disguised in costumes that shed hobo patches and Indian feathers with each step, the boys approached the squat little house on the hill. We girls traipsed behind them, tripping over billowing skirts.

"What's keeping us from taking two candy bars?" Teddie asked.

"Nothing, I guess," Fred said.

"But what if she catches us?" That was Markie. He was a scaredy-cat dressed as a vagabond—no different than he always looked save for the scruffy penciled-in beard and the traveling pouch tied to a stick.

"She can't even see us, you big dummy," Evie said.

"You get it? She's blind," Judy deadpanned.

"But what if she isn't for real blind?"

"Yeah," Kenny said. "Maybe she can see out of one eye."

"If we take two candy bars, the second one might be poisoned," I said.

"That's stupid. What's she going to do—write a number two on the poisoned ones?" Freddie asked.

As it was, none of us took more than one except Markie. He bagged four—two Snickers bars in one hand and two Pay Days in the other.

Because The Blind Woman Within hadn't answered our knock, we agreed that most likely she lie abed with broken limbs, nasty bruises, and assorted lacerations oozing with greenish goo—injuries inflicted, we imagined, while wandering blindly about her house bumping into walls, upsetting furniture, and falling down the basement stairs.

❧ ❧

I coveted the cotton candy cottage at the bottom of the hill, situated well-away from the road. Its matching outbuildings and corresponding garage were ever so

69

tidy and trim. I stood before the pink house for hours—admiring the color scheme and hoping to charm the folks who occupied it so they might deed their house to me when they died. Likewise for the shiny new Chevrolet that replaced their old one in September of every year. At an unpredictable hour of the night, I imagined, the former model disappeared from the driveway to places unknown, and a new car took its place. The lawn got mowed, the flowerbeds weeded, and the shutters got a fresh coat of paint. Such chores were clandestinely accomplished when prowling children were fast asleep in their beds. The owners of the cottage, no doubt, were nocturnal zombies who went about their business at nightfall and retired to bed at dawn's early light.

∽ ⌇

The Bee Man, The Blind Woman Within, and The Zombies in the pretty pink house were the unknown people, the private people—our neighborhood's misanthropes. The folks we'd never seen despite much peeping and prying could be lumped together with one common factor. None of them had kids that we could play with.

But then again, maybe their children were chained in attics or cellars awaiting sleuths like us to free them.

On the Road Again

Those who hated him were far and few.
Those who liked him were loyal and true.
There was nobody in-between.

But that was okay with my father. He disdained ambivalence. Dedicated, hardworking, and exacting, he expected others to be the same way.

Dad was an engineer on the Great Northern Railroad, and talked in rail-speak. He drove freight trains over the Cascade Mountains between Seattle and Wenatchee, headed down the Pacific coast from Seattle to Portland, or switched boxcars at Bayside and Delta Yards in Everett where we lived. He was proud to claim the title of fastest *hoghead*, but lightning speed didn't get him home in time for *beans* every night.

Deadheads. Layovers. Five times out. Two times. I didn't understand the language, but when the phone call for *first out* came, Dad pulled on his gray coveralls, grabbed his leather grip, kissed my mom, and was back on the road again. We couldn't predict when he'd be home, smelling of diesel fuel and cigarettes. And then, it was straight to bed no matter the hour, and tiptoeing and shushed voices for us. Upon arising, Dad regaled us with stories involving switchmen who threw the wrong switches, red blocks ignored, train wrecks, derailments, and brakemen who slept on the job.

We snooped through Dad's leather grip, running fingers under the numbers in grease-smudged time schedules that made no sense. We flicked his railroad lantern on and off. Four freckled noses sniffed the red flares that looked like sticks of dynamite. Brass switch keys were tossed from hand to hand. Sitting on Dad's feet and hugging his legs, we beseeched him for another story. With one child seated atop each foot, he gave us a bumpy ride to the sofa where he amused us with another tale.

But then, the telephone rang.

It was Dad's call to work.

He was back on the road again.

෴

When Dad was away from home, we seldom quarreled, squabbled, or crossed our mom.

"Just wait until your Dad gets home," she threatened whenever we misbehaved.

Although unruly children in our neighborhood were often disciplined with a thrashing, my father's lickings were legendary. Our cries could be heard ten miles away.

But when Dad came home and all was well, he loved to spend time with his kids.

෴

"Got a surprise for you," Dad hollered out the window as he wheeled his pickup into the drive, grinning as he tapped the horn.

We dropped crayons half-melted from the afternoon heat onto dog-eared coloring books, jumped the cement steps, and dashed to the truck.

"Stripped these out of a boxcar," he said, indicating the pickup bed with an expansive sweep of his arm.

Massive sheets of cardboard that had lined the boxcars were heaped in the bed of his truck. Although it lent an air of squalor to our yard, Dad helped us make tipsy cardboard houses all over the front lawn. We propped the walls together while Dad secured the corners with friction tape. Doors and windows were cut out with his hunting knife. He showed us how to attach a peaked roof, and then taped a cockeyed chimney atop it. We each got our own private hut.

We remodeled and rearranged our wobbly dwellings all over the yard until thundershowers reduced them to mush.

❦

Dad played hide and seek with us on a rainy day, concealing each of us in our turn. He emptied a cupboard, stuffed Evie inside, and then rearranged canned goods and cereal boxes around her. I got hidden beneath the dirty clothes pile, while Ted was concealed in the linen closet. He perched Markie atop a door that was open to the wall. None of us thought to look up. None of us could find him.

Oh, what a knack Dad had for locating unlikely and hard-to-find lairs!

He truly took delight in his children.
And oh, how we relished his attention!

∽ ⌒

I lifted the picture from the box and studied the black and white photo.

A boy my age posed beside a pony. A stubborn cowlick stood his pale bangs on end. He had a crooked grin, big freckles, and his pants were too short. I could tell he loved that pony.

The boy was named Sonny. *My dad.* I knew that without asking because of the freckles splotched across his cheeks and nose. I had freckles just like them.

I turned the photo over and over in my hands.

If that boy had lived on Jennings Road, I would have been his friend, I thought. *It's too bad he's a grownup now.*

Window to our World

"You broke their window," I accused Freddie as we distanced ourselves from the Smith's house with lightning speed. He emptied his pockets of fist-sized rocks as we ran.

"I did not."

"Did too."

"Did not." Freddie paused at the top of the hill, huffing. He grinned. "I broke *two* of them."

∞ ∾

Mr. and Mrs. Smith lived in a stately two-story near the end of Jennings Road. The house was painted pristine white, and touched-up every year. Black shutters ornamented its sparkling windows.

Kitty-corner across the road, Leo's moss-covered shack neighbored theirs. Summer and winter, black smoke belched from a stovepipe atop its tin roof. The front door wobbled and wouldn't stay closed. Its windows, murky with mold, were cracked. There was an outhouse around the back, and a distillery hidden somewhere in the tangled woods behind it.

The Smith's home rose up from the middle of a manicured lawn—the only lawn on Jennings Road undotted by dandelions. Dazzling flowerbeds bordered the walks. A weed wouldn't have the courage to sprout in their yard. Mr. Smith hoed the flowerbeds daily.

Leo, conversely, parked his pickup in his muddy front yard. Slimy planks thrown down willy-nilly served as sidewalks. They threaded around piles of lumber and broken household appliances, proceeded past heaps of empty beer bottles and sundry car parts, and then circled back to his door. Stinging nettles grew rampant right up to the walls of his shack.

We often wheeled our bikes across the Smith's green turf just so Mrs. Smith would have a reason to rap on the window, or, better yet, so Mr. Smith would be provoked to pursue us with hoe in hand.

Leo we left alone.

∞ ∞

Mrs. Smith had borne two sickly sons. Neither of them ventured outdoors. I sometimes saw their outlines—pale ghosts that floated behind the sheer white curtains that enshrouded the windows upstairs and down.

I didn't know their names.

I didn't know how old they were.

For a certainty, I'd never seen them at school.

I often wondered how they filled their days.

∞ ∞

"If the little one gets even a tiny scratch," Freddie told me, "he'll bleed to death in a minute. That's what Leo told my dad."

"What's wrong with the other kid?"

"Something awful. I don't know."

Both of my big toes were stubbed and bloody, with one toenail ripped half-off. Scratches on my legs and arms intersected like crossroads on a highway map. Two knees and one elbow were skinned and scabbed over. Mosquito bites had been itched until they bled.

I looked over at Freddie. He bore wounds much like mine.

The little Smith boy would bleed to death in a minute, I thought, *if he ever tried to play with us.*

All at once, my world tilted, and I sat down hard. I felt as faint as a ghostly child keeping watch behind veiled curtains. Seized with fear and horror, I hugged my belly and moaned.

"The windows," I rasped. "The windows."

The sparkling panes that Freddie had broken the previous week unexpectedly had come to mind.

My buddy hovered above me, vaporous and out-of-focus. "The windows?" Freddie said in a voice ten miles away.

"The windows," I again repeated. "You know? The ones you broke?" I blinked my eyes. "I hope that kid wasn't cut by the glass."

Belly Button Blues

"Show us your belly buttons!" our playmates demanded, acting as if my siblings and I were exhibits in a circus sideshow, and they held admission tickets.

Bloated umbilicals were a family trait that had elevated the Cleveland kids to the status of circus sideshow freaks. Proud of our singularity, we flaunted our deformities to friends and strangers alike. Everyone wished to have a button as wondrous as ours, we thought.

Because I so loved my belly button, it came as a shock when my big brother Teddie announced that our abnormal attachments should have been fixed when we were newborns to make them conform to those of "innie" babies.

"You just wait, Treesie. They'll cut off our belly buttons before we grow up," he warned.

"But I don't want to be a Commoner!" I cried.

∽ ❧

Five kids squeezed into the backseat of the station wagon. Three more sprawled in the carry space behind it. Picnic baskets filled the gap in the front seat between

Mom and Winnie. Baby Sister Susie drowsed on my neighbor's lap.

"You kids calm down now," Winnie warned, "or we'll wheel this car around and head home."

But how *could* we sit still? We were on our way to Forest Park where swings, crossing bars, slides, teeter-totters, monkey bars, a merry-go-round, and a wading pool awaited! Peacocks strutted about the park—eager to be chased and plucked of their feathers. There were two bears in a smelly cage—hungry for the likes of us.

So we squirmed in our seats for the half-hour ride, and then eight children exploded from the station wagon and took off in as many directions. Mom balanced Baby Sister on a hip as she lagged behind us. Winnie lugged the baskets and claimed a picnic table.

We ran willy-nilly for hours, pushing play equipment to its limits. But when Hostess fruit pies, Fritos corn chips, cream-filled Twinkies, and jam sandwiches made with Wonder bread were withdrawn from wicker baskets, we abandoned monkey bars and slides and converged on the picnic table. Pricey, store-bought baked goods were a novelty to us. We thought they tasted even better than the delectable cookies, pies, and loaves of yeast bread that our mothers baked at home. After relishing each mouthful of factory-baked fare, we rushed off to play some more.

∽ ∾

I touched the clouds with my toes as I pumped my swing higher and higher. My pigtails lifted. The white sun glowed. Maximum velocity had been attained.

I orbited the moon and then zinged to Mars. Earth, a jewel in the galaxy, was a million miles away. When my thoughts returned to home, I pumped the swing even higher to get there.

Arriving back on terra firma, I surveyed my environs—Forest Park.

Everything around me had changed.

Nothing was normal.

Something was wrong.

I gave my head a hard shake, and then wandered the playground confused.

When neither Momma, Winnie, playmates, nor siblings could be found, I sat on a swing, toed the dust, and cried.

I can disappear and no one will miss me. I can hide and never be found.

In a car piled with picnic baskets and tired children, nobody noticed that I'd been left behind.

It seemed like hours before they came back.

∾ ∽

My hair was brown.

My eyes were green.

I dressed in cast-offs and hand-me-downs.

Nothing about me was exceptionally striking—aside from my belly button. Eye-popping and grotesque, it demanded to be recognized. Unlike me, it would not be forgotten.

I lifted my blouse and beheld my beloved, bulbous button. No matter the cost, I vowed to protect it from any quack who might cut it off.

The Secret Life of Mrs. Belt

The aroma of home-cooked food permeated the kitchen as Mrs. Belt bustled about her stove. Each of three burners on the range heated a cast iron pot bubbling with something savory and scrumptious. I lifted each lid—chicken and dumplings, green beans with bacon, and cinnamoned apple sauce. A pot of coffee perked on the fourth burner.

"Would you have a cup, dear?" Mrs. Belt asked, reaching for a potholder before lifting the aluminum percolator off the burner.

"Yes, ma'am, I would."

That was the extent of our conversation, and it had been so since I'd known Mrs. Belt. I didn't mind though. She was smiling and cordial to scruffy little waifs like me—and generous with her cookies besides.

Mrs. Belt arranged snickerdoodles still warm from the oven on a plate. She filled porcelain cups with coffee. After slopping the steaming brew over the edge of his cup, Mr. Belt slurped it up from the saucer beneath it.

"That's the only way to drink it," he advised.

I spooned as much sugar into my coffee as I wanted. If the sugar bowl came up empty, Mrs. Belt was ever ready to refill it. An inch of warm, wet sugar remained in the bottom of my cup after I'd downed the last of my drink. My finger passed from cup to mouth as I swiped up the remains.

"Help yourself, Missie."

I loved it when Mr. Belt called me Missie.

Nudging the plate across the table with a thumb, he urged me to eat another cookie. Even though it was midsummer, he made inquiries about my studies at school. He spoke about his grown sons who lived in California, but never used their names.

I eyed the wide staircase off the kitchen that led to the second floor. Each son had been given a room of his own, and oh, how I longed to ascend the stairs so I could poke through their belongings! I envisioned model airplanes hanging from the ceiling in the oldest son's bedroom, and a bug collection atop a shelf. Field guides and bird books rose in tidy stacks upon his bedside table. Maps of faraway places like California had been thumbtacked to the walls. The other son, I decided, was athletic and outdoorsy. A basketball, baseball bats, football pads, and a hockey stick were strewn willy-nilly about his room along with grass-stained uniforms and wet bath towels. The outdoorsy son treasured his baseball cards. He had a bigger collection than any other kid in his class.

"The boys don't come up north much, and seldom in the summertime," Mr. Belt remarked.

Mrs. Belt refilled his cup and smiled. She met my eye, and then nodded at the cookie plate.

"Go ahead, Missie. Eat them all," Mr. Belt encouraged—and I did.

I asked to use the bathroom, even though I didn't need to. On some visits, I even asked twice. With the door locked tight behind me, my eyes took in the pretty room's features. A bottle of perfume with a foreign label took center stage upon the counter. It was hard to imagine that my plain-featured neighbor would use it. I fingered the pretty bottle, and then gave my neck a thorough misting. Fine, white hairs clung to the bristles of a silver brush. I pulled them out, washed them down the sink, and then tidied my bangs and the tips of my braids with its matching comb. A bar of pink soap next to the sink smelled so fruity, I ran my tongue across it—twice. My cheeks got a coating of face cream, my lips a touch of red. Before leaving the room, I gave the toilet a flush so Mrs. Belt wouldn't suspect what I'd been up to.

On my short walk home, I considered the details of the sturdy, brick house that Mr. Belt had built for his quiet wife before the birth of their sons. The porch was wide. The door was solid. The windows had shutters that really closed. Everything about the house bespoke of its durability and soundness. Even the furnishings and fittings inside it—cast iron pots, heavy coffee cups, knotty pine cupboards, and a rugged farm table—were practical. After musing upon that, I brought to mind the dainty bathroom within the well-built walls of the house. With its pink fixtures, plush linens, and rose-covered curtains, it seemed disturbingly out of place.

Mrs. Belt wore neither lipstick nor perfume, and surely did not arrange her hair with a silver brush and comb! A heavy hairnet held fast in place her tight, untousled curls. Attired in a drab housedress, flesh-colored stockings, a checkered apron, and sensible black shoes, she looked just like every other old lady on Jennings Road.

Yet Mrs. Belt had a silver comb and brush set, red lipstick, and perfume from a far-off land! It made me wonder about the covert life that she might be inclined toward when nosy children weren't poking about. Perhaps on my next visit, an opportunity to peek inside her closet and dresser drawers would arise.

A Snowstorm in July

"You kids'll nickel and dime me until there's not a penny left," Mom complained as she dropped a coin into each of our palms. "I'm not made out of money, you know."

We quickly closed our fists. Asking for pocket change was all in the timing. We made tracks for the door before Mom changed her mind.

"Now just one minute, you little rascals!"

I tightened the fist that held my dime.

"What do you say for that?" she asked, smiling at her budding beggars.

"Thanks Mom!" all four of us chimed.

"And don't forget to look both ways before you cross."

We hurried outside, banging the screen door behind us.

The privilege of crossing Emander Road on my own had been bestowed upon me when I'd turned five—but not before a traffic test. Mom apprised me of the dangers of a hasty crossing, and then manned a post on the corner while I honed my traversing skills. Emander was a dangerous and busy byway. Up to six or seven cars might toodle by every hour. The driver of each vehicle, of course, was bent on running over careless children.

So, grasping Markie by the hand, Teddie looked one way while I looked the other.

"Everybody set? Let's go!"

We dashed across the two-lane road.

The proprietor of Midland Gardens, Mr. Cannon, looked mean and cranky—but he wasn't. He presided over the cash register and oversaw the wall of candy to the left of the checkout counter—six long shelves filled with Look bars, Big Hunks, Mars bars, Three Musketeers, Bit-O-Honeys, Hollywoods, Tootsie Rolls, and Almond Joys. My favorite was the Sugar Daddy—luscious caramel on a stick. When the temperature rose over eighty, I left it to soften on our picnic table for an hour, and then sank my teeth into the top and twisted it into a spiral.

"How long does it take you to spend five cents?" Mr. Cannon would grumble whenever I opted to spend a nickel on penny candies instead of a chocolate bar.

A whole hour might tick away while I sat Indian-style assessing the mouth-watering merits of each lowly sweet that would set me back only one cent.

A fireball, a gumball, or a miniature marshmallow cone?

Candy lipstick, a jawbreaker, or a licorice mustache formed of wax?

Smarties, a cinnamon bear, or candy cigarettes of varied brands?

Before scattering a nickel's worth of penny candy across the checkout counter, five weighty choices challenged my brain.

But Mom had given each of us a dime, and that meant only one thing on a hot summer day—Popsicles!

Bursting into the store, we each displayed the silver coin gripped tightly between two fingers. Mr. Cannon knew our spending habits. He managed a curmudgeonly smile, and then waved us off to the frozen food case.

The freezer, always in want of defrosting, reminded me of wintry days. I lifted the lid, boosted myself up, and leaned my entire upper body into its frosty depths.

Just that sudden, it was winter. I shivered in the cold.

∽ ∾

Mittened, muffled, and decked out in scratchy wool, we stomped a path through the snow in rubber galoshes that were either too little or too big for our feet. Kids sallied forth from every direction with one destination in mind. The Jennings Road hill was recognized by every child in the local environs as the ultimate sledding spot.

Before the carousing commenced, however, we set up our battle lines. Our rival claimants to the hill were Chevys, Fords, and Buicks—their tires clad in snow chains designed to churn through ice and compact snow while fishtailing up or down our hill. To discourage their passage, a barrier of massive snowballs barricaded the road. We patted together mounds of snowballs to pitch at any car that dared to breach our wall. The younger ones were assigned battle stations. Only after our boundaries had been defined, our arsenal built up, and our strategy outlined, could dozens of children converge on the hill.

Although deprived in other ways, we Clevelands were the only family that owned two full-sized sleds—

Flexible Flyers with precision steering action and steel runners. Holding his sled to the side, Teddie ran ten yards, threw the sled down before him, and then dove onto it belly-down. Dozens of sleds raced with him down the hill—careening, toppling, or swerving out-of control and then into a ditch or a mailbox post.

Because kids were abundant and sleds were scarce, we often laid one child atop the other—three kids on a sled and another to push. The pusher jumped onboard at the crest of the hill, sometimes rolling both captain and crew off their sled and into the path of another.

By compacting mounds of snow, Fred and Teddie had built up a series of snow jumps. When a sled went airborne, the ride was more rousing than a roller coaster. One bump came after the other—and oh, how we flew down the hill! With four passengers per sled, one child offloaded on every bounce. Avoiding ejectees required lightning reflexes, nerves of steel, and quick wits on the part of the captains of the other sleds.

Those awaiting their turn for a ride made snow beds in the rounded ditch at the top of the hill. Our beneficent neighbor, Mrs. Belt, handed out cookies and sometimes cocoa over her half-buried picket fence. With its dusting of snow, the sturdy brick house at the top of the hill looked like a gingerbread cottage. Sweet-tempered Mrs. Belt, in my mind's eye, became the hungry witch in Hansel and Gretel. The cookies she offered would plump me up, and then she'd throw me into her oven and eat me for dinner. Giving no mind to that outcome, however, I always ate more than my share.

After partaking of cookies and cocoa, we lounged on our snow beds with hands beneath heads—cracking jokes and bad-mouthing our buddies. There were snowmen, snow angels, snowballs, and snow forts to make as soon as we rested up. We engineered crisscrossing trails leading nowhere through snowy front yards.

And then, "Car!" someone would yell.

"Man your stations!" another would holler.

Our frostbitten band formed a line three-deep obstructing the road, each with a snowball in hand.

Good-natured drivers who lived at the bottom of the hill were persuaded to turn around in the Koenig's driveway to reach home by a roundabout route. Those who lived directly on the hill, however, were implored to exit their cars and make their way home on foot.

Some of them obliged.

Most of them didn't.

"Aw, c'mon mister. Can't you just walk?" Freddie pleaded.

"I'll give you a ride on my sled," Ted offered.

"We'll carry your grocery bags."

"I'll shovel your walk."

"You can have my nickel."

"I have three pennies!"

"I'll give you a Matchbook car." That was Kenny. His Matchbook cars were so dear to him, he thought they would buy anything.

The hardened adults who dared to cross us were heckled, jeered, and pelted with snowballs. Hunched over their steering wheels with eyes fixed on the road ahead, they plowed through our barriers and proceeded down the hill while dozens of children shouted insults. Because we'd iced the road with buckets of water, the spoilsports often veered their vehicles into the ditch.

"Serves you right, mister!"

Freddie gave orders to let loose with a volley of snowballs.

Exiting his car, the driver shielded his face with an arm. "You kids better watch out. I'm calling the sheriff on you!"

"See if we care!" That came from Teddie who really did care knowing he'd suffer a licking if Dad got wind of our insurrection.

But instead of the sheriff, the county sand truck wheeled onto Jennings Road. It bore down on our sledding hill.

"Hey, I'm just doing my job," the driver told us, shrugging his shoulders as his truck lumbered past us—scattering sand in its wake.

We assessed the damage wrought by both car chains and sand, and then repaired the bare patches with mounds of snow tamped down with shovels. Sparks flew off the steel runners when a sled hit a bare patch that our unruly road crew had missed.

As dinnertime approached, mothers stood on icy porch steps calling their offspring home. Not one of us gave them attention, and soon our moms ceased calling.

The sky darkened.

Low clouds spit out snow.

We couldn't feel our fingers.

Our toes grew numb.

Snot froze beneath our noses.

Sodden clothes caused us to shiver.

But we didn't care.

It seemed like midnight before we trekked home.

⌀ ⌀

"You kids find what you're looking for yet?" Mr. Cannon hollered down the aisle.

Green Popsicle in hand, I raised myself out of the freezer and back into summer.

Whether Popsicles or penny gumballs, I always picked green. Markie, of course, couldn't make up his mind. To save him the bother, Evie thrust a red one into his hand.

Mr. Cannon relieved us of our dimes and then ushered us outside.

Knowing that Mom would warn us to "keep that sticky mess out of my house," we lingered before the wide window closest to the store's main door. Teenagers claimed the other window—a domain where we dared not tread. The boys smoked Chesterfields, spit, swaggered, snorted, and came close to picking a fight. The girls sat on the windowsill looking pouty or bored while assessing the boys on the sly. They smacked Bazooka bubble gum and sipped Pepsi Colas and 7-Ups.

Seated on the lowly sill relegated to youngsters, we kept a close watch on the teens as we sucked, bit into, or licked our frosty treats. We hoped that they'd soon leave so we could snag their empty pop bottles. Regardless of the three-cent return deposit, they never failed to leave them behind.

Customers who exited the store became recipients of our scrutiny too. When they rummaged for car keys in pockets or purses, we held hopes that handfuls of change might scatter across the lot. We were ever alert to retrieve it. When the older boys stubbed out their cigarettes and began pitching pennies, we anticipated further plunder.

Already I was imagining the treats I might buy with those pennies and nickels while Mr. Cannon thrummed his fingers on the counter and impatiently looked on.

If You Ask a Stupid Question...

The questions our mothers often put before us were inexplicable and confusing. Some had no reasonable answers, yet if we responded, "I don't know," we likely would be told, "*I don't know* isn't an answer." Other replies to their probings might incriminate a sibling or friend—and no one wanted to be a tattletale. The rest of their inquiries were just plain dumb. In such cases, if we said what we really thought, we'd be confined to our rooms for a month.

∽ ∾

What do you expect me to do about it?
Since when did you become the boss?
Do you think I'm stupid?
What kind of excuse is that?
Are you even listening to me?
Did I hear you right?
Where were you when the brains were passed out?
What do you have to say for yourself?
What do you think you're doing?
Why did you do that?
Do you think I'm blind?
If you didn't do it, who did?
What were you thinking?

Were you even thinking?
If everyone else jumped off a cliff, would you?
How many times do I have to tell you?
Can't you see I'm busy?
Did you even hear a word I said?
Do you think I care?
Who told you that?
Who put you up to that?
Where did you get that?
Is that the best you can do?
Where do you think you're going?
What are you up to now?
Have you looked at yourself in a mirror today?
Do you think I didn't hear that?
Who put you in charge?
Did I ask your opinion?
Do I have to draw you a picture?
You're not much good at that, are you?

෴

Because the responses to their varied questions were either implicating, obvious, or a "smart ass" remark, we seldom produced an acceptable answer. If we finally did conjure up a reply, however, our inquisitor most likely would ask, "Now what kind of answer is that?"

Leftovers and Leavings

Our galomping Great Dane, Prince, dwelt in a dusty and dung-littered pen in a corner of our backyard. When the exuberant dog occasionally was uncaged, we took turns riding on his back. It didn't take long for the bounding beast to unseat us.

The dog's appetite was kingly, and kibble was costly. For that reason, Prince's twice-daily portion of dry dog food was supplemented with scraps from The Penguin Café. The women who waited tables at the popular lunch spot scraped the leavings from the customers' plates into gallon cans, and then set them in the alley at the end of the week for pickup by my dad or mom.

The Penguin Café in downtown Everett was owned and operated by my great-uncle Bill and my auntie Virgie. Occasionally, they invited us in for a burger when we ventured into town. While waiting to be served, I ran my palms over the gobs of chewing gum that had been stuck beneath the table by the café's patrons. Evie and I waddled salt and peppershakers in the shape of twin penguins across the Formica table.

Emerging from the kitchen, my great-aunt passed a mug of root beer to each of us kids. Held in place by condensation, a paper-wrapped drinking straw adhered to the side of each mug. We wiggled in our seats, awaiting Auntie's signal.

"Are you ready, kids?" she asked, grinning.

We looked to our mother. She graced us with a nod.

"Yes!" we said, all at once.

Auntie produced a straw from her apron pocket and peeled off a tiny end of the paper covering to expose the tip of the straw. Putting it to her lips, she puffed out her cheeks and shot the wrapping across the café—a signal for the rest of us to follow suit. Extra straws were withdrawn from her pocket and distributed around the booth. A dozen skinny paper cylinders soon littered the café floor. Businessmen looked up and chuckled, and then went back to their coffee and pie.

Although I relished the rare treat of dining at The Penguin Café, the repugnant aroma of the restaurant scraps that I dished up daily to our dog Prince ascended unbidden to my nostrils the moment the waitress set my burger and fries before me. I conjured up the smell of half-eaten club sandwiches, coleslaw, chicken-fried steak, tapioca pudding, meatloaf, banana cream pie, potato salad, turkey gravy, Jello, cottage cheese, BLTs, and mashed potatoes—an unsavory mélange of café fare muddled together and crammed into a can. A sour taste arose in my throat. I made a beeline for the bathroom.

That came out well for Prince, at least. He devoured my barely-touched burger and a side of fries for dinner that night.

Babysitter Blues

"But it's the Fireman's Ball!" Mom pleaded after dialing up the seventh potential sitter. "Please... you're the last one on my list."

Even though the teen's dad was a firefighter, the girl showed no pity. She bluntly declared, "I'm busy."

At the top of every babysitter's Blacklist, THE CLEVELAND HOUSEHOLD stood out in bold, block letters—underlined and exclamation-pointed. Our reputation was widely renowned. At school bus stops, lunchroom tables, and slumber parties, the names of my siblings and I resounded as our victims commiserated, compared injuries, and exchanged harrowing accounts of the mayhem that ensued the moment Mom and Dad pulled out of our drive.

One sitter, desperate for pocket change, was given a run for her money when she dared to take us on. We screamed like wild banshees as she chased us around and around the house—over the sofa, under the table, and up and down the stairs. The contents of her purse went into the toilet, and then we overflowed both sink and bathtub. When we ran out of steam at bedtime, the sitter tucked us in with a grateful sigh. But the moment she settled upon the sofa for some peaceful TV viewing, we bounced out of bed and renewed our rampage. When

Mom and Dad arrived home, the sitter fled in such a hurry, she forgot to collect her pay.

Another unsuspecting simpleton arrived on our doorstep with suckers and storybooks meant to tame us. Seated on the couch beside her as she paged through the picture books, we innocently tongued our treats. When the suckers became quite gooey, we tangled them in her hair.

Based on detailed observations of the Cleveland kids, a cerebral sitter wrote a school report on deviant child behavior. Her incredulous psychology teacher accused her of embroidering the facts. The girl received a failing grade, and was removed from the honor roll at Cascade High.

Our favorite sitter, Violet, lived directly across the road. She was the only teen who cheerfully braved an evening with rascals and reprobates. Violet's big brothers were rough and untamed—setting the bar for her many beaus. Harley and Bruce went to school only when they wanted, drank Leo's moonshine, drove souped-up cars with wide backseats, and had girlfriends that Dad said would "wind up in trouble." Crouching within the trailing tendrils of their enormous willow tree, we beheld them with wonder as they tinkered on their cars.

Because Violet lived in close proximity and conveniently could betray us, we took on the form of angels upon welcoming her into our house. We ate our TV dinners without a food fight, played a game of Uncle Wiggly without wrangling, and brushed our teeth and went to bed on command. When my brothers were fast asleep in their downstairs bedroom, Violet ventured up the attic stairs. Sitting cross-legged on a bed, she paged through a stack of teen magazines while Evie and I snooped through her purse and tried on her lipsticks. Smacking double sticks of her Juicy Fruit gum, we quizzed her about the photos of teenaged boys displayed in the clear plastic sleeves within her wallet.

"Has he ever kissed you?" we asked, pointing to each one in his turn.

Oh, how it electrified us when Violet revealed that she had kissed them all—and more than once! In lieu of a bedtime story, she divulged details about her dates and the wily ways of young men. Violet was so sought out by the hearty fellows, she seldom had a free night to watch us.

Obliged to settle for sitters less vibrant than Violet, we broke every household rule that our parents had enforced upon us while the beleaguered sitter attempted to keep us in hand. And then, knowing that we'd catch it for misbehaving, we entreated her on bended knees not to tell our folks. Pitiful and repentant, we described horrific punishments that might be inflicted upon us if Mom and Dad found out—amputations of arms, legs, tongues, and ponytails using a rusty saw or a carving knife.

Whether compassionate or foolhardy, not one of them ever squealed. Because of their kindly discretion, Mom never figured out why babysitters quickly declined almost every time she sought to engage one.

The Girl

The girl lived on Stockshow Road in a house with shutters askance and a weed-filled yard. Because she had five big brothers, she could hold her own in a squabble, I thought, without sullying or wrinkling her blouse. Swarthy and reckless, the brothers toted BB guns and ate six-inch night crawlers on a dare. Nary a child on Jennings Road had the guts to provoke them.

～ ～

The girl's smile was playful, but wary. Her features were sharp, but soft. Elaborate braids tied together with ribbons held long, brown hair back from a face that bore neither birthmark, blemish, nor freckle. Her clipped and clean nails were polished with pink.

The girl wore sweater sets embroidered with flowers. Her play clothes never were patched. She changed her clothing from one day to the next, and nothing was soiled or scuffed.

I imagined that she bathed every night in a tub filled with bubbles.

I imagined a mother unbraiding her hair, and kneeling beside her to pray.

I imagined the girl in a room all her own. It was painted pink, of course.

∽ ⌒

The girl was born with an arm that had grown from shoulder to elbow, and then—it stopped! At the end of the arm were two long fingers that had neither joints nor nails. If we paid the girl a nickel, she let us peek up her sleeve. For a dime, we could squeeze her two fingers.

∽ ⌒

The girl never gained my pity, in spite of her handicap.

After all, didn't every one of us kids look for a way to earn a nickel to buy five pieces of penny candy? Yet the girl filled her pockets with nickels and dimes every day. In the face of adversity, she was resourceful. Because of that, I coveted her misfortune and secretly wished that I could cut off an arm, and then grow a new one back just like hers.

It shames me to say that as long as I was wishing, I requested a nose without freckles, unfrazzled hair, fingernails polished pink, and store-bought clothes besides.

The Bee Man

Ash trees with low-lying branches flanked the entrance to The Bee Man's realm. His house, unseen from the road, was tucked beyond a curve in the drive. Cars neither entered nor exited his driveway. It was overgrown with lank, matted grasses.

No one amongst us had set eyes upon The Bee Man. We'd seen neither house, bee, nor beehive besides.

The last house on Jennings Road—the house where The Bee Man lived—held a secret that begged to be told.

The same could be said of The Bee Man besides.

Delightful and dangerous facts that we might uncover about the recluse both thrilled and terrified us. Speculations as to The Bee Man's height, girth, features, and demeanor were debated and tossed about.

Evie imagined him as timid and shy—but given to occasional fits. "He screams like a banshee," she said, "then he bites off his tongue and spits it out all bloody."

"Don't worry. He glues it right back on," Judy assured the wide-eyed Kenny, Markie, and Little Kathy.

I held to the notion of a disfigured recluse—bee-bitten, slack-jawed, and ungainly. "He claws at his bee bites and eats the scabs."

"And then the stings get infected and they squirt out green goo," Freddie said.

"Well, The Bee Man *has* been stung 137 times," Teddie concurred. "That's what Leo told Denny."

My brother's friend, Denny, lived across the road from Leo, our neighborhood's source of outrageous and appalling newsflashes.

If Leo said it, no one would doubt it.

If Leo said it, we took it for truth.

But even without promptings from Leo, we spun fantastic tales about The Bee Man of our own.

"His sixteen kids all got stung to death," Evie said.

"So did his wife," Ted added.

"But was The Bee Man even ever married?"

"At least five times," Freddie swore.

At the height of our conjectures, The Bee Man changed from husband and father into a merciless, cold-blooded outlaw who bred bees that stung on command.

"He's wanted in a hundred states," claimed Kenny.

"He can't be," Judy said. "There aren't that many states in the whole country."

"How many are there then?"

"Ninety-nine, so there!"

Because The Bee Man kept hives that housed 137 bees, nobody was inclined to set foot on his range. But, driven by boredom on a hot summer day, we determined to spy on the fabled hermit at the end of the road. Mindful of his 137 bees, we dressed in winter coats, long pants, mittens, and hats, and then wormed through the brambles that encroached on his yard.

Sweaty, sticky, and parched for want of water, we endured the sun's white heat while awaiting The Bee

Man's appearance. With dirty windows and a leaf-littered porch, the house loomed before us—forbidding, forlorn, and unfriendly. During the course of our stakeout, we never caught sight of The Bee Man. Nor were we swarmed by his bees.

With all that honey for the eating, we agreed, *he's too fat to squeeze through the door.*

Disheartened and dying of thirst, we abandoned our post and straggled back to the road.

Leo was rooting through a heap of car parts—flinging them every which-way—as we passed before his shack.

"Why you kids dressed like that on a day like this?" He wiped the sweat off his forehead with the hem of his shirt. "You're all gonna die of prostration."

"That's better than getting stung by 137 bees," Kenny said.

Leo gave us a befuddled look.

"We've been spying on The Bee Man," I said.

"The Bee Man?" Leo threw back his head and let out a laugh. "Why child, didn't nobody ever tell you?" He shook his head and chuckled again. "The Bee Man's been dead twenty years!"

The Lonely One

T eddie ground his teeth. It made a chilling racket.
Evie slurped and sucked her thumb.

Markie was prodded toward the toilet at midnight, but his bed was still wet in the morning.

Baby Susie woke up and squalled.

Mom usually got up and calmed her.

Dad snored.

And me?

I was the quiet one—neither tossing, turning, nor twisting the covers. As I remained wakeful well beyond midnight, the nighttime noises of my parents and siblings afforded me a bit of protection.

And oh, how I needed protection!

∽ ∾

The objects in our attic bedroom took on sinister and menacing forms the moment the lights went down. They concealed, I was certain, The Lonely One—a fearsome phantom who never made his presence known, but lurked nearby all the same. His ghoulish gang of crawly creatures crept across the windowsill and clawed their way up the curtains in full view of my horrified eyes. The entourage of gruesome beasties might pounce upon me without warning, but it was the unseen Lonely One who posed the gravest threat. In the melancholy gloom of darkness, I awaited his gory attack. If he caught me by surprise, I'd be dead for less than a minute before he'd pick my bones clean, snap them in two, and suck out the marrow.

∽ ∾

Only once did I cry out to my mother, but then, embarrassed, I held my silence when she answered my call.

I confided my fears to Auntie Sis instead. She wrestled with qualms like my own.

"If it can't be seen, if it can't be touched, then it can't be real either," she assured me, but both of us knew better than that. "Seeing is believing," she continued. "But don't believe everything you see."

Auntie spewed out so many contradictions, I never knew what to think.

"The Lonely One grows bigger in the dark," I told her on another occasion.

She gave me a flashlight, but the batteries were dead.

"Keep your eyes shut, kiddo," Auntie next advised. "If you do that, he can't possibly see you."

That night, eyes screwed shut, I tried to pray. But my belief in monsters overpowered my faith in a protective God.

I cowered beneath my covers, trying to remember the words to the lullaby Auntie had sung to me years before—ten little monsters, each doing something horrid and fiendish.

Bad idea!

The hair-raising jingle scared me half to death.

I heard Teddie downstairs, coaxing Markie toward the toilet. If I was bold enough to bolt down the stairs and join my brothers, I could bask in the glorious light of the bathroom's single, bare bulb. I'd snuggle down in Markie's bed—never mind that he'd soon soak the sheets. But The Lonely One, I knew, would be fast on my heels before I even hit the stairs.

So with fingers linked across my chest in expectation of the end, I lay still upon my bed, eyes closed—and listened.

Evie slurped as she sucked her thumb.

Baby Susie woke up and squalled.

Mom padded to her crib to calm her.

Dad snored.

Teddie ground his teeth.

Markie's bedsprings twanged.

I pretended to pray.

The restless lullaby soon made me drowsy.

I got my ration of forty winks.

Wardrobe Failure

I stripped the gown off its padded hanger and slipped it over my head.

Next, I accessorized with baubles and belts.

Finally, I stepped into three-inch heels.

Arrayed in Momma's dancing dress, bedecked in her jewels, and wobbling on three-inch heels, I preened before the mirror.

An ardent admirer, more dashing and devilish than any Prince Charming, held forth his hand as he approached me.

Behold the comely maiden!

As I twirled around and around, a heel caught the hem of my gown.

And…

There was the sound of ripping fabric.

There was a gasping intake of breath.

There was a panic-stricken and hasty inspection.

Oh Lord! Heaven help me!

I had ripped that lovely dress.

My face paled. My body froze. Slowly, oh so slowly, the garment slipped off my shoulders and pooled at my feet.

Mom's going to kill me!

If I tallied up the times that Mom had reason to take my life, I'd be condemned to the fiery furnace more times than I could count. Such a fate would be well deserved, but Mom, to my good fortune, wasn't given to such extremes.

I stepped out of her wobbly heels and gathered up the gown. The fabric was pale green organza—quite daring and almost see-through. Twinkling rhinestones studded the fitted bodice. The skirt, fully gathered at the waist, floated off Momma's hips.

She looked like a wood nymph when she went to The Ball, I remembered, envisioning her exit out the door on the arm of my dressed-up dad. They left behind four children and a baby to terrorize the babysitter.

The Fireman's Ball, a fund-raiser hosted by volunteers in the rural district, was a gala and much-anticipated fete. Each female attendee strove to outshine and out dress her rivals, while the menfolk, I imagined, gathered around a crystal punchbowl. The fruit juice held within it likely had been spiked with moonshine bequeathed by Leo, our neighborhood's hooch distiller.

I held the dress at the hemline and examined the ragged tear.

Acquiring a spool of green thread to match the gown would be impossible, I feared. Even if I chanced upon one, I'd still have to thread the needle and learn how to sew. Before I succumbed to despair, however, a realization made me rejoice.

This is last year's ball gown!

Relieved and happy of heart, I returned the heels to the shoe rack.

Mom gets a new dress every year for The Ball!

I snapped off the earrings, unclasped the necklace, slipped five bracelets off my wrist, removed three dinner rings, and unbuckled one belt studded with rhinestones and another one heavy with pearls.

She won't even know this one's missing!

I hung the padded hanger at the back of the closet.

I can't wait to try on next year's gown!

Bunching fifty yards of silk organza firmly against my chest, I peeked out the bedroom door.

I heard Momma humming in the kitchen.

The coast was clear.

I dashed to the attic stairs, ascended them by twos, and then stashed the gown under my bed.

At an opportune time—the sooner the better—I would bury Mom's frock in the woodlot where a real wood nymph would be sure to find it.

Flora

An enormous rhododendron with purple blooms grew in the center of Freddie and Judy's lawn. Covering nearly the entire front yard, its outer limbs bent clear to the ground. Brown leaves littered the floor beneath the huge shrub and gave off a musty scent. The inner leaves were covered with mold. With branches that stretched to the second floor of the Koenig's house, we imagined it a million years old. Circling around and around, we scrambled through the limbs of that oversized bush for hours—heedless of scrapes and scratches.

Mountain ash trees lined the back end of the Koenig's driveway. In the fall, birds got drunk on their fermenting fruit. We filled galvanized buckets with the orange berries, climbed up a tree, and rained them down on passersby's heads—most often those of our tagalong, younger siblings. When we perched on the fat branches of the pine tree next to the road, we used a similar tactic. Our weapons were pinecones sticky with pitch.

The border between the Koenig's house and the rental next door was bounded by an unruly, overgrown hedge. We tunneled through limbs covered with waxy, smooth leaves in search of secret hiding places. Diving from one yard into the other through the gaps, we finished with a somersault.

∾ ℮

The Koenig's house was the only one on Jennings Road that had a doorbell. For that reason, whenever we slept out in someone's backyard, it became the target for midnight bell ringings.

The tall, thin house with its steep-pitched roof looked sinister in the darkness—no matter that it was painted white. We sprinted across the lawn to the darkened house and bounded up the porch steps. Each of us in turn rang the bell, and then, holding back shrieks and giggles, we scrambled to our hideouts in the fabulous hedge. Although we feared a beating if our moms and dads found out, we hoped that Frank Koenig would stumble onto the porch, hair wild and eyes afire—hopping mad, shouting threats, and shaking clenched fists above his head. I secretly wished that he would locate a child—not me—and throttle him until he was senseless. No matter that Frank failed to perform such theatrics, the prank never lost its thrill.

Even the Koenig kids, Freddie and Judy, took part.

They took the lead, in fact.

Through the Wringer

Mom with Evie, Markie, and Teresa
in the backyard

"Don't go in the garage," Mom sternly warned me. I stepped back from the door.

"There's stuff in there I don't want you messing with," Dad added. "You could get hurt."

Those admonitions—firmly embedded in my mind—harkened back to when I was small. They never had been dislodged.

Keep Out!
No Trespassing!!
Do Not Enter!
Stay Away!!!
Danger!
This Means You!!

The garage, I came to believe, was a breeding ground for bloodcurdling creatures. Even grown men who drove diesel locomotives across the Cascade Mountains cringed at the prospect of facing the heinous, wailing creatures within its walls. The aforementioned train engineer, my father, even declined to park the family car in the garage. Not wishing to undermine his hero status in my eyes, Dad held to the excuse that he was unable to force open the wide, warped doors. Whether the buckled doors were truly unopenable and askew, I did not venture to test out. I feared what might lurk behind them.

The forbidden building would remain untracked, uncharted, and unexplored—at least by me— forevermore.

∽ ∾

A walled-off room inside the garage served as my mother's washroom. She entered that room but once a week. Unmindful of menacing and malodorous monsters, she went about her washday chores with gay and careless abandon.

Life-threatening hazards notwithstanding, one of us young ones—usually me—might be called upon to carry a wicker basket of wet clothes from the laundry room to the wash line in our backyard. I did so with uncertainty and caution. The dank and musty room with its solitary cobwebbed window was opulent in its decrepitude and squalor. It smelled of cat pee, bleach, Tide detergent, and other indistinguishable and vile odors. So as not to make eye contact with a brutal beastie, I kept my eyes to the floor, snatched the wicker basket, and bolted outside.

To further imperil her offspring, Mom might ask one of us—usually me—to help her wrestle the wringer washer.

"You'll have to do this yourself someday," she blithely quipped. "Might as well learn the ropes now as ever."

Although shaken and unnerved, I manned a position opposite my mother. She extracted sopping clothing, sheets, and towels from the belly of the wringer washer, and then fed them through two moving rollers set close together that wrung the water from them. It was my job to catch the clothing and linens as they passed through the rollers. During the course of my internship, the wringer washer often came alive, walked across the cement floor, and belched out sudsy, gray water. Fortunately, my post before the rusty relic was nearest to the door. Many times, I fled the washroom—wailing and as white as a bed sheet.

When I wasn't fretting about the hulking washer before me or the cagey creatures that might be creeping up behind my back, I worried that Mom's fingers might get caught between the wringers where they would flatten both hands and arms. Even more horrific than that, what if her whole body got drawn through the wringers and then flopped flattened into my ready arms? If the worst occurred, I decided, I'd pin her to the clothesline until she revived.

With the washing accomplished, Mom clothes-pinned the wrung out towels, white socks, flowered panties, and other sundry clothing and household linens on a sagging wash line in the backyard, and then propped it up with a pole. When she doubled bed sheets across the line, Evie and I pulled the two sides apart and tunneled through them.

Once the clothes on the line were dry, Mom forged on to the ironing. The mangle, a pressing machine, was another unwieldy gadget designed to maul or maim my mother. The name itself—The Mangle—bespoke of danger.

Mom sat bravely before the beast, positioned a pillowcase between a heated presser and a padded roller, and then nudged a pedal with her foot. The presser closed down on the roller with a frightening hiss. At that point, my mother, befuddled and broken from wrestling the washer, might unwittingly catch her fingers between the two parts. Before she came to her senses, not only her fingers, but also her hands and arms would be charred or reduced to ash. Yet, ever courageous and bold, Mom fed piles of cotton sheets into The Mangle. She controlled the beast so well, she could deftly pass even shirts and dresses through it.

All day, and well into the evening, Mom relentlessly mended, folded, and then stashed our clean garments in closets and dresser drawers. We all pitched in to make up our beds with crisp, cotton sheets. But before us kids even had washed hands, face, and feet in the sink before donning pajamas, Mom collapsed upon her unmade bed and immediately dropped off to sleep.

Considering the rigors of washday, it's no wonder that all of us wore the same clothes for a week—no matter if grass-stained or grimy. If Mom ever attempted to dress four kids and a baby in clean clothes every day, she would be forced to take up residence in the washroom where the wringer would run day and night. And then, because of Mom's fearless and plucky nature, she soon would persuade her new roommates, the ghouls in our garage, to help out with the added washing.

Haunted House For Sale

Grandma Mable and Grandpa Cleve
with Teddie

Mrs. Nester lived alone in a house engulfed by a full-grown monkey tree, unpruned shrubs, and stickery holly bushes. Seven well-tended rows of raspberries grew between our houses. There were another six rows on the opposite side of her property—thirteen rows in all.

The only time we saw Mrs. Nester was during raspberry season. On those infrequent sightings, the only sign of her presence was a black pointed hat.

"She has to be a witch," Teddie whispered as we crept as near to the wire fence as we dared.

The black pointed hat moved along the tops of the raspberry canes as our neighbor picked her way down the row.

"I wonder what she looks like," Evie said.

Mrs. Nester's face, I imagined, was green and disfigured. Her fingers were clutching and long. She had bristly hair, a pointed chin, and warts all over her nose. While we slept, Mrs. Nester wandered about our woodlot collecting salamanders, swamp water, beetle bugs, bat wings, mushrooms, and mice. Her gleanings were ingredients for a potion that bubbled in her cauldron day and night.

If another woman had lived in that house, our crafty gang would have crept into a back corner of her berry patch intent on stuffing our mouths with sun-warmed berries until we all got bellyaches.

If another woman had lived in that house, she would have welcomed children into her yard, and then served up raspberry shortcake with generous dollops of cream.

But Mrs. Nester was not that woman.

No doubt in our minds that the plump raspberries on prickly canes that drooped over to our side of the fence had been poisoned by our neighbor.

Never were we tempted to eat them.

∞ ∞

The moon was full.

The night was dark.

Mrs. Nester was dressed in black.

There was a sound of squealing brakes.

There was a scream, abruptly cut off.

There was a thump.

There was a plop.

The car left skid marks on the road.

∞ ∞

Several days after the speeding car launched Mrs. Nester into the afterlife, my brother Markie chanced upon a broom in the ditch.

All of us screamed at once. "The witch's broomstick!"

Markie dropped it, and we fled.

Who knows what devilish mission Mrs. Nester would have accomplished if she hadn't been thwarted by that heroic, hit-and-run driver?

∽ ⌒

The weekend after Mrs. Nester passed away, Grandma Mable and Grandpa Cleve paid us a visit.

"It's too bad you can't buy Mrs. Nester's house, even though it's probably haunted," I said.

"Well, maybe Grandpa and I should walk over and give it a look."

The prospect of our beloved grandparents living right next door thrilled us kids, of course.

"If Grandma and Grandpa move to Jennings Road, they won't need an outhouse no more," Evie said.

I smiled and crossed my fingers. I need not worry ever again about falling into the lime-dusted depths of their outdoor toilet.

Closing my eyes, I sent a prayer in the direction of the heavens above.

Oh, if only You might persuade my gram and grandpa to move into a haunted house!

∽ ⌒

After my grandparents bought Mrs. Nester's house, Grandpa plowed under almost all of the raspberries—saving only one row along the wire fence between our houses. No more need we worry that they were poisoned.

In no time at all, we wore a path between our houses. When Grandma walked over, she leaned on a pointed, wooden pole.

"Got 27 slugs along the way," she announced, leaning her pole against the back of the house.

My stomach turned over at the sight of those shish-kebabbed slugs on the end of her stick, their pale yellow guts spilling out.

"That's 167 this week, and I haven't even walked home yet."

Gram lent an ear to our problems, pulled out our loose teeth with pointed pliers, and put pin curls in our hair. She whistled when she did the dishes, or recited old-timey poems. Evie and I spent sultry afternoons trying to tame her cats. We didn't have to guess their names or wonder how to tell them apart. They were all calicoes, and Grandma named every one of them Minnie.

Grandpa sat in his rocking recliner, read the dictionary, and memorized five new words every day. After signing his name with a flourish, he sketched an American eagle below it. If we coughed long enough and hard enough, he'd reach into his pocket and give us each a pink peppermint lozenge.

"It simply amazes me that you kids have lived so long with such severe cases of whooping cough," he'd remark between our fits of coughing.

After we promised to look both ways before we crossed Emander Road, he gave us thirty cents and dispatched us to the store. The quarter was for chewing tobacco. The nickel was for us.

∾ ℘

Hidden within the branches of an enormous snowball tree, I imagined living in a house just like Gram and Grandpa's. I'd have a bowl of cookies atop the refrigerator, wilted flowers on the table, kitchen towels embroidered with the days of the week, and a pair of pointed pliers. My husband, whom I fancied would be Freddie, would fill his shirt pockets with peppermint candies. Our calico cats would all be called Minnie. Despite the efforts of our twenty children, not one of them would ever be tamed.

The Teenie Tiny Village

"Read us a story about the Teenie Tiny Village," we begged. "Please, Momma, please. The Teenie Tinies!"

My sister Evie and I wiggled into our positions on the couch, sandwiching our mother between us. Opening the book, she whisked us off to a warren in the forest inhabited by people no more than four inches tall. They lived in abandoned leather boots and rusty coffee cans, harnessed black beetles to a plow, and embarked on fantastic adventures upon the backs of field mice and songbirds. As small as the little folks were, they faced many dangers. But they were most resourceful, and the forest animals often came to their aid.

I loved the Teenie Tinies.

I wanted to be small just like them.

Oh, how I wished to inhabit their world!

❧ ❧

I built a miniature abode beneath the roots of a stump, and another amongst fiddle neck ferns. I made diminutive shelters out of twigs and bark and imagined myself inside them. With soft, green mosses upon my floors, I had no need of a bed. With butterflies, bugs, and field mice about, I had no need of a friend.

∽ ∾

The nymphs and elves that I communed with lived in luxuriously appointed underground or treetop dwellings. They dressed exquisitely but with eclectic abandon.

I was the one they trusted.

I was their beloved.

I was ever flawless in their eyes.

They showed themselves to no one else.

∽ ∾

I hid under tables, inside the snowball bush, and under the steps. I befriended the feral cats in Grandma's garage. During Hide and Seek games, no one could find me. When my playmates gave up and commenced Kick the Can, I remained in my hiding place.

∽ ∾

Each night I made a wish to God, even though I had reason to doubt Him.

Make me littler every day

so no one will notice—

so no one will miss me when I'm gone.

Upon arising the next morning, I gauged my height, and lost my faith even more.

∽ ∾

I was average in weight.

I was average in height.

I was neither magnificent nor mediocre.

And yet, I felt oh-so-little inside my skin—trapped inside a body that was much too large for my teenie tiny self.

Career Training

An abandoned chicken coop perched on a small rise near the back of the grassy field behind the Koenig's garage. Fluffy red feathers caught in its splintery floorboards were all that remained of that backyard venture.

Freddie and Teddie, handy with a hammer and nails, took charge of the remodeling when we converted the coop into a clubhouse. The Jennings Road kids scoured every outbuilding in the neighborhood, and then pestered the owners for tools and building supplies. Every backyard had a pile of scrap lumber. Every father had jars of nails, screws, and bolts lined up across a shelf in his dusty garage. Cardboard boxes stacked against the walls brimmed over with useful gadgets.

"Can we use Frank's drill if we put it right back?" Markie asked Winnie as she pulled weeds along the back of her house.

Because Markie was so gullible and willing, we dispatched him to procure our tools. His pure and guileless smile charmed even the most hardened curmudgeons on Jennings Road. Hammers and saws that we'd left rusting in the rain might be returned days or weeks later, yet he was seldom turned away empty-handed.

In a corner of the chicken coop where the floor had rotted out, we excavated a basement. The boys heaped galvanized buckets with dirt. The girls emptied them outside. Upon completion, the basement accommodated up to eight children. Its opening was disguised with a secret trapdoor.

The boys hammered a makeshift ladder onto a wall, and then built a loft on one end of the clubhouse. It was entered through a hinged trapdoor. Trapdoors were essential features in a bona fide clubhouse. They were used anywhere and everywhere we could think to put one.

Likewise for ropes and pulleys. From our perches in the rafters, we transmitted messages written in secret code from one end of the clubhouse to the other by pinning our notes to an old clothesline and then launching them forth by means of two pulleys. We conveyed cargo from upstairs to downstairs using a bucket, rope, and pulley as well.

After being bossed by the boys for weeks while serving as their unskilled assistants, Judy, Evie, and I were given a task of our own. We were to insulate the entire clubhouse by lining the walls with broken-down cardboard boxes gleaned from Midland Gardens Mercantile.

At last we'd been granted access to hammers, nails, and knives! We set our hearts to the project. It never occurred to us that the insulation was entirely useless. The glass in the windows along the front of the chicken coop had been broken out years before.

When we could think of no further building projects, we spent hours lounging on the slanted roof of the clubhouse with hands tucked beneath our heads. We pointed out the shapes of elephants, dragons, and floppy-eared rabbits in the puffy clouds.

"Right there—see? It's a giraffe," Fred said.

Evie shaded her eyes with a hand. "Looks more like a dinosaur to me."

"No it doesn't. It's an alligator standing up." That was Markie.

"Whoever heard of an alligator standing up?" Judy said, sounding much like her mother Winnie.

We flung ourselves off the roof peak into a steaming heap of rotting grass clippings that came from the Koenig's lawn.

When we shouted out the windowless windows, our voices echoed against the cement block walls of the grade school across the field and over the road. We hollered until we were hoarse.

We harvested bucket after bucket of orange berries from the mountain ash trees that bordered our woods to hurl from our rooftop stronghold at any enemies who might be lurking about. When enemies failed to invade our clubhouse, we pelted Kenny, Markie, and Little Kathy instead.

The boys tied a rope to a rafter, and then we took turns hanging each other. When my execution came around, I stood on the upturned bucket. Freddie fastened the noose around my neck. To keep myself from choking, I grasped the rope above my head with both hands.

"Guilty as charged," the hangman Freddie boomed.

That was Teddie's signal to kick out the bucket from under my feet. I was saved from strangulation only moments before my arms gave out. Fred grabbed me by the legs and held me up while Teddie freed me from the noose.

The clubhouse was used as a practice site for our firefighting exercises too. Freddie was old enough to mow their lawn, so he had access to the gasoline. He lit the matches and set the fires. The rest of us manned a bucket brigade from the Koenig's outside water spigot to the clubhouse. The fire almost got out-of-control only once. Our terrified faces were smudged with soot, and we all got our eyebrows singed off.

"I'll only use half as much gas next time," Freddie told his crew.

But when Winnie got wind of the blaze, our firefighting careers were extinguished. For an eternity of seven days, entrance to our lair was barred.

Visiting the Aged and Infirm

Elderly relatives and friends of the family often received house calls from my kindly mother. She tidied their living rooms, washed up the dishes, and changed the sheets on their beds. Hoping to instill compassion for the unwell and wobbly in our malleable minds, my siblings and I were obliged to accompany her.

"You'll be old like them someday," Mom said.

Not one of us kids believed her. Old people were born that way, we thought. Just like Moms and Dads were. Just like kids and babies.

∾ ∽

Peggy's ramshackle one-story had been drawn deeper into the spongy ground of her blueberry bog every time we paid a call. My siblings and I awaited the day when we'd arrive to discover that both house and blueberry bushes had been sucked into the underworld.

Ailing and unsteady, Peggy was at least two hundred years old. When she answered our knock, little Markie—held fast by Mom—reluctantly turned his cheek for her welcoming kiss. She smothered him between bounteous breasts. Although Markie kicked and hollered as he worked himself free, he was the only one of us Cleveland kids that Peggy liked.

Peggy's aged and arthritic dog—a wheezing pooch with a matted coat—provided the only entertainment within her house. All of us were loath to touch him, but touch him we must as the determined dog blindly made his way toward us, bumping into end tables crammed with bric-a-brac. Clumps of his fur covered the carpet—home to many of his fleas as well. Anticipating doggy breath, we pulled tee shirts over our noses and breathed through our mouths.

Because there was nothing better to do, we displayed our finest manners during Mom's sojourn with Peggy that always lasted some fifty hours. That amounted to the four us sitting in a line across her sofa with hands folded upon our laps while we silently counted to sixty—*some three thousand times.*

Both Peggy and her pooch were not long for this world, we dared to hope.

∽ ∾

Mrs. Dehnhoff was Grandma Mable's best friend, and they checked in by phone each day. For the most part, they dissected the lives of the folks who worked at General Hospital, a Hollywood set location of their favorite daytime television drama. Speculations as to what would happen—or what they wished would happen—on the next episode were tossed about, cast-off, and then tossed about anew. The doctors at General Hospital were licentious and lusty. Both Gram and Mrs.

Dehnhoff nursed secret longings for the men in white, I thought.

Mrs. Dehnhoff lived on Lord's Hill in Snohomish on the ranch below where Grandma and Grandpa had lived before moving to Jennings Road. Even after her husband died, Mrs. Dehnhoff remained on their ranch. She spent her days baking oddly-shaped cookies from Old World recipes that had been hand-carried on a transport ship bound for America hundreds of years before. A silver platter, heaped so high with cookies that they toppled off, dominated her kitchen table. In no time, we'd laid waste to them all.

Mrs. Dehnhoff's flowerbeds, unkempt just like Grandma's, brimmed with blossoms of riotous colors and weeds gone-to-seed. Aside from the bouquets that she picked for my mother, the flowers had been given over as a feast to the slugs that shared her garden plot. Before piling back into the station wagon, we tromped through Mrs. Dehnhoff's untidy orchard so she could pick a bagful of wormy apples for us to take home.

❧ ❧

Great-Uncle Emmett, an aged, wrecked relic, lived on the topmost floor of a tall, thin house that rose up from a narrow gully. To reach his garret apartment, visitors needed to cross a skinny, wooden footbridge. The bridge was rickety. My siblings and I were reckless. Yet we always feared to traverse it.

In exchange for the casseroles that Mom delivered to his door, Uncle Emmett filled the back of our station wagon with wicker baskets heaped with prize-winning produce from his immaculate garden in the gully.

A rickety bridge and prize-winning produce—that's all there was to know about Uncle Emmett. On account of having a greater fondness for solitude, strong drink, and scratchy whiskers, he never had taken a wife.

ॡ ॡ

Four wiggly children prowled Auntie Mildred's crowded quarters while Baby Sister Susie wailed on Momma's lap. Toys, puzzles, and broken gadgets cluttered the teensy apartment. We were allowed to touch everything.

A multitude of plush animals paid homage to Humpty Dumpty who held court on a sofa arm. He was dressed up like a dandy in his red plaid suit. None of us would own up as to who had smashed in his plastic nose. We didn't have to. Markie always took the blame for everything that went awry.

As we poked around the one-cook kitchen, we emptied a candy dish heaped with cheap chocolates so old they were white on the edges. A yellow duck on the table pooped out jellybeans when you stroked its back.

"Mind your fingers," Auntie warned as we snooped through the cupboards and drawers. Each of them contained a baited mousetrap.

French doors led into her bedroom. We dove into the middle of an unmade bed covered with rumpled blankets. Evie and I riffled through piles of movie magazines while Ted and Markie perched on the window seat, upsetting knickknacks that had been broken and mended countless times. They shattered an ornament every visit.

Auntie urged us to sit at the table, and then passed around plates of dessert. The cake, riddled with eggshell shards, was covered with lovely swirls of frosting heavy on shortening and light on confectioners' sugar. We politely forked it down before bidding our dear auntie goodbye.

⌒⌒

Despite the tedium of Mom's visitations, we came to grow fond of her wilted and wobbling old friends. It saddened me that soon they might die.

"It'll be strange when there's no more old people in the world," I told Mom after we'd departed the house of a benevolent, bedridden chap.

"No more old people?" She looked at me askance. "What do you mean, honey?"

"Don't you know, Momma? When all the old people die, there'll be no more left for us to visit."

Famous Last Words

Up and down Jennings Road, the tidings conveyed from mother to child could be expressed in less than thirty phrases. Because their responses to our ineptitudes and actions were so predictable and standard, we wondered if there might be a special training school where mothers learned such jargon. In any given situation, we could almost guess what they might say.

∽ ⌒

Because I said so, that's why.
I said "no" the first time.
If that's what you thought, then think again.
I'm not telling you twice.
I don't care if her mom lets her do it, I'm not her mom.
You're getting too big for your britches.
Wipe that look off your face.
If I've told you once, I've told you a thousand times.
You'll have to ask your dad first.
Go to your room and don't come out until I tell you to.
Crying won't make it better.
Don't talk to me like that.
Do as I say, not as I do.
I don't want to hear any more of your excuses.
I don't care what he said.

I don't care what he thought.
I've just about had it with you.
I hope you learned your lesson.
I'm the boss around here!
Don't sass me.
You deserve a licking for that.
If you ask me one more time, I'll send you to bed.
The next time I have to ask you, you're getting a
licking.
Just wait until your dad gets home.
I'll get back to you about that later.
Get back here. I'm not through with you yet.
Look me in the eye.
Don't look at me that way.
You better not be lying.

ᘛ ᘚ

We seldom had the nerve to sass our mothers, but if we could tell them once, we could tell them a thousand times. "Don't talk to me like that! And now go to your room and don't come out until I tell you to."

Pretty Things

Grandma Grace
with Prince

Grandma Grace arrived on a boat from Scotland with no money and no one to keep her. She married a sailor boy.

I never met that mariner. I didn't even know his name.

∞ ∾

I knew little about my grandma, although she lived not so far away.

She called my sister Duckie.

She taped our drawings to the fridge.

She cleaned the homes of elegant ladies.

She was Mother to my mom.

∞ ∾

Grandma set a lovely, wee table each time we paid a visit. Mindful of our manners, Evie and I sipped milky tea with plenty of sugar from exquisite, flowered teacups. When Grandma's budget allowed her to splurge on cookies, they came from the finest sweetshop in downtown Seattle.

∞ ∾

Although destitute and quite poor, Grandma Grace loved pretty things, and, for that, I remembered her best.

Her living room was filled with cardboard boxes stacked nearly to the ceiling. I imagined the pretty things they might contain.

Bath salts in crystal containers.

Lace-edged parasols.

Dusting powders with fluffy, pink puffs.

Silken dressing gowns.

Leather-bound books embossed with gold.

Ostrich feathers.

Fingerless gloves.

Flirty fans.

Silver hair combs.

Sachets scented with bergamot.

If Grandma would just delve into those boxes, I thought, *she never would be poor again.*

∽ ∾

Grandma Grace died when I was small.

I missed her Spartan, teatime fetes.

Yet I still felt happy every time I thought about a grandma who had a fondness for pretty things.

She'd be pleased to be remembered like that, I thought.

Friends from Afar

To cut down on their telephone bill, my mom and dad shared a phone line with four other households. The "party line" essentially made it impossible to make and receive calls. Whenever my parents picked up the receiver and made ready to dial, another person on our party had taken access to the line. Mom and Dad groused and grumbled, yet the annoyance was fully their fault because they had opted out of paying extra for a private line.

"I thought she'd never get off the phone," Dad complained after waiting for two minutes to place a call.

"That woman's been yakking at least an hour," Mom grumbled later that day, plunking the receiver onto its cradle.

"You better make that call before someone else ties up the line," she frequently advised.

If the need to use the phone was urgent, one of them might pick up the receiver and then slam it back down again several times in quick succession—not letting up on the assault until the other party cut short their chat.

"Well! I guess someone more important than me needs to make a call," the person might wryly comment before hanging up.

Having limited access to the phone was only one annoyance that pained my parents. In addition to that grievance, they aired complaints about its unremitting ringing. When anyone on our line received an incoming call, every other phone on the line rang too. To differentiate the calls, each household was assigned a distinct sequence of rings. Ours was five short rings in quick succession. That meant that if our phone chimed only once, twice, thrice, or four times, someone else on the line was getting a call. With various members of five households receiving calls, our phone rang at all hours of the day and night. One out of five calls, on an average, might be for us.

On the plus side, if certain persons were inclined to curiosity—and I was—they need only pick up the phone on another household's ring to eavesdrop on their conversation. With that in mind, the phone company took pains to assign party lines to folks who likely weren't acquainted—families two roads to the north, south, east, or west perhaps.

Such a policy greatly distressed me. I *wanted* to know who was speaking. Hiding a person's identity was an unnecessary precaution bordering on paranoia, I thought.

Not having so much as a nodding relationship with anyone on our line, however, didn't deter me from giving an ear to their chats. At any hour throughout the day, I could quietly lift the receiver and garner fascinating details about the lives of people I didn't know and very likely would never meet.

"If you don't quit nosing in on my calls, I'll report you to the phone company," one of my vociferous victims might warn if they suspected that I was listening in.

Such trifling intimidations didn't daunt me. By the time they hung up, looked up the phone company's number, and then picked up the receiver to dial it, another member of our party would be tying up the line.

❧ ❧

Although identities had been denied me, I knew by name every person who shared the line with our household. I became privy to the names of their children, their in-laws, their workmates, and their dog as well. By means of a telephone line, I formed endearing connections to those on our party, so it sorely perplexed me when they belied such a bond with me. Because of the bold nature that possessed me only when on the phone, I barged right into their conversation, and then engaged my audience with pleasantries, opinions, and advice. My unsolicited but caring comments were entirely underappreciated.

My parents, on the other hand, assigned cruel nicknames to my friends from afar. The Old Blister, The Windbag, Motor Mouth, and The Old Biddy were amongst the more pleasant. The longer each remained on the line, the livelier became their nickname—astonishing and wondrous strings of words that were not of common usage.

I frequently gave thought to what nicknames might have been bestowed upon my mother by those who shared our line—or, worse yet, names that might brand my father. Impatient and commanding, when he picked up the phone and it was in use by another, he shamelessly demanded that they hang up.

"Lady, you've been yakking long enough. There's other people might need to make a call."

Upon hanging up, the offending party quite likely lifted the receiver to eavesdrop on my dad.

∽ ∾

Nobody knew your family's practices and problems better than those who shared your party line.

"I've a mind to tell The Old Blister what to do with those kids of hers," Mom grumbled after several attempts to place a call.

"I've heard enough about The Windbag's bowel habits to last me a lifetime," she complained some time later, banging the receiver down.

"I'm pretty sure that woman who called Mr. Big Shot wasn't his wife," she wagered on another occasion.

Apparently I wasn't the only one who enjoyed listening in on private calls.

∽ ∾

While Mom did up the breakfast dishes, I picked up the telephone. At that hour of the morning, Ring #2, Sally Ann, carried on lengthy and detailed discussions with her friend Shirley—gossip too bewildering and remarkable to miss.

"And then Dotty told her if she didn't keep her big mouth shut about it, she'd damn well shut it for her—excuse my French," Sally Ann reported.

"Lord Almighty! It's not like everybody doesn't know what her husband's been up to," Shirley replied.

"I saw the bastard tiptoeing in the house at two in the morning last night. The light was on in their bedroom, so I knew the fur would fly."

"Oh my God! Dotty had a black eye when I saw her at the store this morning!"

"Last time the snake pulled a stunt like that, she fought back with a baseball bat."

"I don't know why she doesn't just give him the heave-ho."

"Well, you know she's pregnant again, don't you?"

"Oh Lord! Now for sure I know she's crazy!"

I sank into the soft cushions of the overstuffed chair and dangled my legs over the armrest. The phone receiver rested comfortably between my cheek and shoulder. Feeling worldly-wise and all-knowing, I absorbed the news of the day.

The Writing on the Wall

A black telephone with a rotary dial hung on Grandma Mable's kitchen wall. A pen dangled from a worn length of string thumbtacked beside it. Grandma didn't keep a pad of paper near the phone on which to jot down messages from her callers. She scribbled everything on the wall instead.

I twirled on a swivel chair reading the disjointed phrases, phone numbers, times, and dates until they became a dizzying blur. Only then might I decipher the profound prophesy hidden within my grandma's graffiti—the writing on the wall that my Sunday school teacher had told me about.

They drank wine, and praised the gods of gold, and of silver, of brass, of iron, of wood, and of stone. In the same hour came forth fingers of a man's hand, and wrote over against the candlestick upon the plaister of the wall of the king's palace: and the king saw the part of the hand that wrote. Then the king's countenance was changed, and his thoughts troubled him, so that the joints of his loins were loosed, and his knees smote one against the other. The king cried aloud to bring in the astrologers, the Chaldeans, and the soothsayers. And the king spake, and said to the wise men of Babylon, Whosoever shall read this writing, and shew me the interpretation thereof, shall be clothed with scarlet, and have a chain of gold about his neck, and shall be the third ruler in the kingdom.

I had no aspirations to be the third ruler. Neither had I need for a chain of gold about my neck. *Let thy gifts be to thyself, and give thy rewards to another,* I thought. *But oh, to be clothed in scarlet!* My heart quickened. Oh, to be clothed in scarlet rather than cast-off and hand-me-down raiments that were three sizes too big so I could wear them until I grew into them, and then I could wear them even longer after that.

So I praised the gods of gold, and of silver, of brass, of iron, of wood, and of stone. Because Gram lacked wine in her cellar, I took a nip of the corn whiskey Grandpa had procured from Leo, the covert distiller who lived near the end of Jennings Road.

But no matter if I squinted my eyes, drank moonshine, or spun in the swivel chair until I was dizzy, there was no interpreting of dreams, shewing of hard sentences, and dissolving of doubts.

My countenance was changed. My thoughts troubled me. The joints of my loins were loosened. My knees smote one against the other.

I could not read the writing on the wall!

I could not shew the interpretation thereof!

So from thence and beyond until the end of mine days, I wouldst be hearkened throughout the land as The Wearer of Cast-offs and Hand-me-Downs.

Table Manners

"Get back to the table until your plates are clean," my mom called out as Evie and I made tracks for the door.

Our mother held fast to the notion that children should eat every crumb on the plate put before them. I took exception to that rule. After my brothers had licked their plates clean and clamored for seconds, I generously would have forked over my firsts. Red meat could be masticated in my mouth for hours, and still I found it hard to swallow. But ingesting tough chunks of beef did not assure my reprieve. The vegetables on my plate yet awaited my fork.

Long after Ted and Markie had gone out to play, Evie and I remained at the table. Oh, how we longed to join our brothers, but we simply couldn't stomach our food. We nudged green peas and carrots around and around our plates with a fork—arranging and rearranging them in intricate and artsy patterns. We were convinced that with the proper arrangement, the food would vanish before our eyes. But alas, we never got the pattern quite right.

Clever girl that she was, Ev soon devised a method of ridding her plate of its leavings without consuming so much as a bite. After mashing carrots and peas to a pulp, she spread them like putty on her plate's underside.

"Now there's a good girl," Mom said when Ev tilted up a dish so clean it needn't be washed.

Evie carried it to the sink anyhow and turned on the faucet. Insipid canned carrots and pale, sickly peas went down with the water. She looked my way and raised her brows as if to dare me.

I soon followed her plan of escape.

∞ ∞

Mom's friend Dolores was of a different persuasion when it came to mealtime. Four finicky eaters mapped out their menus, after which Dolores dished up each individual plate as ordered.

"Those kids would starve to death if they were mine," Mom said. "She's crazy to spoil them like that."

But I secretly wished that Dolores was my mother—if only at mealtime.

∞ ∞

"Just push aside what you don't like and eat what you do," Shirley would say if a certain dish didn't match her children's likings.

When foods failed to pass muster—and often they did—the kids filled their bellies with white bread and butter.

∞ ∞

When Freddie or Judy failed to finish their dinners, Winnie served the leftovers for breakfast the following morning. The foil-wrapped plates would be plunked down before them—straight out of the refrigerator. If they couldn't stomach the remains for breakfast, they were served to them again for lunch.

∾ ꙮ

Those amongst us who were required to clean up their plates often grumbled and commiserated. To end our oppression once and for all, we agreed to run away. Carrying knapsacks and bedrolls, we'd strike out on foot—leaving our homes and homeland behind us. My sister Evie proposed a menu both nutritious and tasty to sustain us on our trek—candy corn and jelly beans.

Twilight Games

The sky darkened.

The moon rose.

The stars gave off their faraway light.

One after another, the children on Jennings Road straggled into our front yard. Forming a circle, each child stuck one foot in the center—toes touching together like spokes on a wheel. Freddie tapped sneakered or flip-flopped feet around the wheel to the beat of the rhyme:

"Eeeny Meeny Miney Moe.

Catch a tiger by the toe.

If he hollers, make him pay.

Fifty dollars every day.

And you are not IT!"

The foot touched on IT was removed, and the chant renewed.

"Eeny Meeny Miney Moe..."

The last foot in the circle was IT, and the games began.

We played Statue Maker, Steal the Bacon, Hide and Seek, No Witches Are out Tonight, and Red Light-Green Light.

We played Cigarette Tag, Kick the Can, Red Rover-Red Rover, Frozen Tag, Colored Eggs, and Mother May I?

When we tired of those games, we invented new ones. When we tired of the new ones, we returned to the tried-and-true.

∽ ∾

Although frightening when the moon was full, No Witches Are out Tonight was my favorite game. The chosen hag hid while, eyes closed, the rest of us counted—first slowly, then faster and faster. Upon reaching fifty, we crept from Home Base and spread across the yard chanting, "No witches are out tonight! No witches are out tonight! No witches are out tonight!"

Without warning, the hag sprang from her place of concealment and hunted down her victims. Heinous shrieks, arms that grasped, and fingers that clutched froze the little ones in their tracks. Those tagged before reaching the safety of Home became members of the witch's coven. The hiding and hunting continued until only one fleet-of-foot mortal remained. The victor became the next witch.

Although the sky became darker and our outlines more obscure, we could have played our games until midnight. But long before any child was willing to quit, the mothers on Jennings Road switched their front porch lights on and off and then called through cupped hands the names of their offspring—beckoning us all home to bed.

The Relief Crew

Frank and Winnie Koenig
with Fred, Judy, Kenny, and Little Kathy

There was an understanding on Jennings Road that when one mother's patience ran thin, another one took up the slack. Ragtag bands of children breezed through backdoors and into cozy kitchens, never thinking—and never being asked—to first knock. We helped ourselves to treats from whichever mother recently had filled a cookie jar. If we weren't allowed free rein in certain kitchens, we snitched our goodies on the sly.

"You keep her in the living room. I'll raid the cookie jar."

"Make sure you don't rattle the lid this time!"

"That wasn't me. It was Kenny."

There was a need to be attentive and stealthy. Our mothers had ears like a cat's.

∽ ∾

On rainy days, we gathered in the upstairs bedroom of Fred and Judy's house. We sprawled in a circle on the floor with a pile of comic books within arm's reach. The steady drumming of rain on the steep-pitched roof and the riffle of comic book pages soothed eight squirmy children just as effectively as "nerve tonics" tranquilized certain high-strung or overwhelmed mothers on Jennings Road.

It wasn't long, however, before someone snatched at a Superman comic another child was "hogging."

A tug-of-war broke out. The comic book was torn asunder. There was more grappling, grabbing, and rolling about.

"You're making so much noise up there, I can't think straight," Winnie would holler up the stairs.

That was our cue to move on to the Cleveland house until my mother reached her wit's end.

Upstairs in our attic bedroom, a little phonograph and a stack of 78 and 45 rpm children's records might keep us entertained for an hour. My favorite was "Mike Fink—King of the River." We sang the rollicking tune with gusto at the top of our lungs. We played it over and over and over again.

Oh what a gutsy fellow,
He'll spit right in your eye!
He's gonna live forever—
Born too mean to die!
BORN TOO MEAN TO DIE!!

Another spirited favorite was "Yaller Gold."

I met a gal in Swanee town—
Twinklin' toes and a dancin' gown.
She wasn't for me,
And the reason is this:
She busted my jaw
When I asked for a kiss.
Oh, her lips were red,

And her eyes were bold.

Her hair's the color of yaller, yaller......YALLER GOLD!

Sometimes we played 78 records at 45 speed. That slowed the song down and lowered the pitch of the singer's voice. If we switched 45's to 78, the music resounded at hyper-speed and provoked giddy delirium amongst our ranks.

As we warbled our way through the stack of records, arguments arose as to whose turn it was to choose the next song and who was next in line to put the needle down—not Markie, Kenny, or Little Kathy, of course. The younger ones might scratch a record that had been scratched countless times before.

"You kids better simmer down!" Mom would yell from the bottom of the stairs. "And that means *all* of you!"

Similar expressions abounded amongst the mothers on Jennings Road.

"You're wearing my patience thin."

"I'm not warning you a second time."

"I'll never get anything done with you kids underfoot."

"I can't take another second of your fighting!"

"If I have to tell you one more time..."

"You're walking on thin ice!"

"Can't you kids stay out of my hair for just one minute?"

"You're about to give me a nervous breakdown."

Such phrases cued us to prudently take our leave and move on to another house where we would frazzle the nerves of another mom. Most often, we trooped back to the Koenig's. Having been given an hour's reprieve, Winnie was good for a second go-round. Amongst all of the mothers on Jennings Road, she had the steeliest constitution.

∽ ⌒

Winnie Koenig was constant, complicated, and often commanding. She was an enigma that I could not figure out.

"That is not a laughing matter, young lady," other mothers sternly scolded, one hand on a hip and the other pointing a finger.

Turning red in the face, the child attempted to contain her mirth, or tried to keep from wetting her pants.

But Winnie was not like those mothers. At times, she would burst out laughing when a child dared to act wayward, wicked, or unwise. Her laughter was glorious—like no other sound. It always enlivened my day.

If Winnie felt exceptionally cheery, she allowed eight wired children to play eighty-finger polkas on the upright piano in her living room.

Her husband Frank craned his neck around the corner. Having a mind to kick us all out, he made ready to direct a rebuke to the mob.

"Don't stifle them, Frank. They're composing," Winnie said.

He threw up his hands. "That's not composing! It's decomposing!"

And then, it was out the door for all of us, and on to another house…

The Back Bedroom

My grandma Mable had a place for everything in her house—and that place was her back bedroom. Whether it was a mismatched shoe, a scrap of fabric, leftover knitting yarn, a broken toaster, back issues of Workbasket magazines, or a pan of burnt brownies, if Gram didn't know where to put it, it got tossed into her back bedroom.

Shadows filled that room, smothering and dreary. Curtains of cobwebs, tattered and grimy, swagged its only window. In the center of the ceiling, a bare bulb hung by an electrical wire. A tug of a pull string just out of my reach turned it on. Not wishing to vary the withering gloom, I chose not to strain for the string.

Narrow aisles allowed me passage between stacks of boxes—unlabeled and provocative. As much as I itched to mine the contents within them, the guesswork of not knowing thrilled me even more. I imagined mildewed dancing gowns, a dead man's bones, a Union musket, broken music boxes, tangles of tinsel, love letters bound with a ribbon, moth-eaten sweaters, a king's ransom, snow globes, a Confederate flag riddled with holes, toys with broken inner workings, a mummified mouse, crazy quilts yet unfinished, hair ribbons, hats, and photos of grim-faced relatives dead and gone.

A cot made up for company took up a corner of the room. The sheets were crisp with starch. The pillow was plump with down. A patchwork quilt with embroidered edgings around the piecework topped it off. No matter that the cot was pretty, whenever I spent the night with Gram, I preferred to bed down on the couch.

Smelling of mothballs and mice, a tiny closet opposite the bed contained nothing but wire coat hangers hanging on a clothes rod. They rattled ominously together when the door swung wide. Mindful of baited mousetraps, I squatted in the back of the unlit closet, its door closed tight—waiting, waiting, waiting for something horrendous to happen—or, better yet, an appearance of the mystifying Basil who was spoken of amongst the adults in hushed whispers or behind a hand. Basil was the husband, paramour, companion, or nemesis of Grandma's sister Mildred. Because my siblings and I never had met him, we imagined that he had joined the navy, joined the circus, or joined a religious order. Any minute—if I sat very still—he'd pop in for a visit. But nothing horrendous happened, and the baffling Basil remained at-large.

The back bedroom closet was dark and stuffy. Mice skittered within its walls. The oxygen in the closet's close quarters was all but spent. Soon I would suffocate.

Over the mesmerizing drone of the TV that played from morn until night, I could hear Gram humming the tune to an old-timey song. The kitchen timer beeped. The teakettle whistled. The oven door slammed shut. In sync with the clatter of pots, pans, and crockery, Gram moved about her kitchen. The enticing aroma of peanut butter cookies soon lured me from my hiding place.

Grandma smiled when I joined her in the kitchen. No doubt Basil would join us for tea.

Like God, He was a Mystery

Without hordes of careening kids bounding across the blacktop, the schoolyard was eerie in the summertime. When a breeze set the swings in motion, I imagined ghost children swaying on them back and forth.

Hanging upside-down by my knees from a twirling bar, I picked at a blister on my palm until it bled. My hands were lumpy with callouses from countless circuits on the crossbars and rings. I knew enough tricks to put on a performance.

I'll join the circus when it comes to town, I thought, *and hide out in a wagon until I'm discovered.*

When the ringmaster stumbled upon me, I would thrill him with my act. The lions would roar. The clowns would applaud. Awestruck acrobats would entreat me to join their troupe. My traveling bag would brim with leotards in every color. They would shimmer with sequins, of course.

I swung by my knees ever higher and higher, and then flipped off the twirling bar.

∽ ∾

I took a shortcut through the field behind the Koenig's house to save a long walk home from the schoolyard. Old Mr. Koenig, grandfather to Freddie and Judy, sat on a wooden wheelbarrow next to the path that traversed the golden field. Leaning slightly forward, veiny hands resting on a cane, he lingered in the midst of the field for hours, staring across its matted grasses. Gruff and abrupt, Mr. Koenig addressed me in German and thrust his cane in my path at the last minute in an attempt to trip me. The prank never failed to delight him.

"Thressa," he uttered sternly as I skipped toward him on the path, raising puffs of dust with every footfall.

"Teresa," I repeated, drawing out the syllables of my name in an upraised voice.

He cupped a hand to a very large ear. "Thressa." A comforting chuckle rose within his chest.

When Mr. Koenig stood up, I took his arm. We ambled to his apartment. Any child who passed his way was given store-bought cookies, peppermint candies, or a shiny quarter. If we guessed correctly what was hidden in the hand held behind him, he doubled the prize.

∽ ∾

I knew nothing about the old man with the spotted, gnarly hands. Like God, he was a mystery. He intrigued me, terrified me, fascinated me, and charmed me. I secretly wished that he would die so I could move into his apartment in the Koenig's garage, but then crossed my heart for even considering such a thought.

We can be roommates instead! I decided.

The prospect, however unlikely, of cohabiting with Mr. Koenig fueled my imagination. The quaint and cozy room that I so shamefully coveted had a large window before a breakfast table. It overlooked the Koenig's yard. Oh, how I longed to sit before it as the two of us ate cookies and candies for breakfast and lunch—and possibly dinner too. No sooner than midnight, I'd pull quilts from a cupboard and make up my bed on the couch.

∽ ⌒

When I passed by the following day, the wooden wheelbarrow—unmanned and forsaken—rested in the midst of the field. I was puzzled and confused. When Mr. Koenig didn't answer my knock at his door, I waited on the stoop.

Winnie looked out from her kitchen window, and then disappeared. The side door opened. She walked across the grass.

"Mr. Koenig," Winnie told me, "has passed away." She placed an arm across my back as I faced the vacant field, tears brimming from my eyes.

∽ ⌒

Because Mr. Koenig was smarter and more available than an unseen God, I had given him devotion and honor.

The old man was sage-like and solid—and I wasn't.

He knew all the answers—and I didn't.

Mr. Koenig could have explained all of my wonderings if we had shared a common tongue. He could have lessened my uncertainties.

But then, with startling suddenness, the chair at the breakfast table was vacant when I passed by the window each day. The wheelbarrow stood empty in the field of grass.

No cane to trip me. No arm to take hold of. No one to esteem.

No more cookies. No more quarters. No more peppermint candies.

I missed Mr. Koenig.

It seemed like God Himself had died on the day that my dear friend passed away.

Bedtime Ritual

Markie, Baby Susie, Evie, and Teresa
taking their Sunday bath

My sister had a vile and shameful habit that sorely vexed our mother. Intolerant of nasty leanings, Mom devoted hours of her day—and even lay abed at night—devising schemes to break Evie's inclination. At indeterminate hours throughout the night, Mom crept up the attic stairs—bent on catching her in the act. My unfortunate sister was found out every time.

And what was the sin that so shamed her?

The impenitent child sucked her thumb!

Impelling Evie to cease from sucking would be like forcing me to face my fear of the dark. My nighttime terror was a hidden habit, and I meant to keep it that way. If Mom became privy to my secret, who knows what measures she might adopt to rid me of my dread? The abominable possibilities shook my bones. But poor Evie couldn't hide her secret. The telltale, rough and reddened calouses on the knuckles of her thumbs gave testimony to her deep-seated habit.

To bring my sister to shame, we were encouraged to call her Buckie. Cruel taunting and name-calling, however, didn't daunt my sister—a stubborn and incorrigible child who would suck the whole family into poverty and dishonor when she reached her teens and required braces to straighten buck teeth that stuck straight out. The possibility of financial disaster apportioned a measure of guilt to Evie's shame.

But such tactics proved ineffective.

Our mother's inability to control her young daughter obliged her in time to seek the advice of an expert in the medical field. From his inventory of potions, the pharmacist brought forth a heinous product—concentrated cayenne in a bottle. The tiny vial strongly resembled clear nail polish. It even had a little brush attached to its lid for ease of application. But woe to the woman who might paint it upon her nails by mistake! Her fingertips would likely dissolve. After reading the disclaimer on the label, Mom took care that her own tender skin avoided contact with the vial's fiery contents. Dutiful and doting, she painted Evie's thumbs with liquid cayenne each night at bedtime in lieu of a lullaby. But that scheme failed as well. Within days, my sister had developed a liking for the taste of hot sauce.

Our desperate mother next decided to inflict torture on her second daughter that hearkened back to the dismal Dark Ages. As the light of a full moon illuminated our attic bedroom, Mom withdrew two curious gadgets from an apron pocket—oversized springs with strings attached. How our mother came upon that implement of torture, we might ponder all our lives. We surmised, however, that she had commissioned a demented, down-and-out inventor to produce a device that would squelch Ev's soothing practice forevermore.

The springs were designed to fit over the thumbs, and then tied fast to each wrist with the strings. Any attempt to suckle resulted in an unsatisfactory intake of air. Mom fastened the springs to my sister's thumbs, tied them securely, and then bade her daughters goodnight. Within seconds of her departure, Ev grasped a string between her budding buckteeth, undid the knot, and chucked the spring under the bed. The second contraption soon joined it.

But Mom was not to be outwitted by a seven-year-old. On the night that followed, she painted Evie's thumbs with cayenne, secured the springs with granny knots, and then slipped a sock over each hand and fastened them to the sleeves of Evie's nightgown with a dozen diaper pins. As an extra precaution, she wound ace bandages around the whole works. To our mother's chagrin, Evie had shed her bonds by dawn's early light. She then commenced to suck her thumb in earnest to make up for the wasted hours.

After that, Mom consulted the local Boy Scout Master regarding the useful art of knot tying. Allotting an hour from each busy day, she practiced the craft until soon upwards of twenty different knots were used each night to bind my sister's thumbs. Mom's diligence in that regard left no time for a bedtime story, let alone tucking us in or listening to prayers.

Night by night, my sister became increasingly adept at detangling the knots in order to free her beloved thumbs. Within weeks, she could unloose her bonds before Mom reached the bottom of the stairs.

Regardless of their clashing of wills, Evie one day might thank our mother. She was developing a marketable skill, at least, as she honed her Houdini act.

Teresa's Curse

I studied the picture of my namesake in my father's high school yearbook. The other Teresa stared back through studious, dark-framed glasses. Even though the photo was black and white, I guessed that the young lady's hair was mousy brown and that she'd applied neither rouge nor lipstick. The photo revealed only her torso, but I knew that she sported a pleated, plaid skirt beneath the no-nonsense blouse that was buttoned up primly to her neck.

My father claimed that the other Teresa had marched the straight and narrow—a path that I would follow as well. Matching my step to hers, I'd be a nice girl, a smart girl, and a source of pride to my father.

A boring girl like her, I thought.

I glared at the unappealing picture until my eyes grew dim and blurry. My destiny locked her bespectacled eyes with mine as if to mock me.

The other Teresa was washed out.

The other Teresa was watered-down.

The other Teresa was starched and pressed.

I slammed the yearbook closed and shoved it under the bed.

$\sim \;\; \backsim$

A lively nickname, I decided, *might free me from Teresa's Curse and upgrade my life from dreary to cheery.*

But friends received a scolding when they blithely called me Terry.

"Her name is Teresa," my mother tersely corrected each and all. "Just plain, old Teresa."

The dismal and lackluster name resounded in my ears. It fell from Mom's mouth with a plunk. No matter how anyone pronounced it, no matter their tone or timbre, Teresa simply lacked pizzazz.

I hated my name with all of its unpromising implications.

I hated my father for encumbering me with it.

I hated my mother who squelched the nickname Terry.

I hated the prissy and proper Other Teresa—the girl that I was fated to be.

∾ ๛

Mom had chosen my middle name, Lee, and I loved the sound of that. Lee was Momma's brother who had died when just a boy. My uncle never grew into his fine, strong name.

Lee. I practiced saying it when I was alone.

Lee. If only my friends could call me that!

To escape Teresa's Curse, I resolved to flee to foreign environs where the name Teresa had never been uttered, imagined, or even dreamed about. In that land—Timbuktu or Tallahassee—my new friends would call me Lee.

Roller Derby

A squalling baby flopped on Opal's hip as she plodded up the road. Six children straggled behind her. Opal didn't have a husband. She had another baby every few years anyhow. There were rumors that she was a witch.

To avoid being hexed by the evil eye, my neighbor Diana scrunched down beside me. As we wormed through the spiky foliage of Mom's lily patch, the husbandless woman and her fatherless urchins passed before us.

Because of Opal's dark and unknown past, she captivated and intrigued me. I would have sold my soul to the devil to know her secrets. But Opal's eyes, framed by lashes heavy with black mascara, remained fixed on the road before her. The sun shone through the filmy skirt of her frock, revealing both legs and under panties.

The mothers on Jennings Road reshaped their bodies with stiff girdles and white brassieres. They never left the house without a slip on. Opal, however, was shamefully slipless! Her panties looked scanty besides. I wondered if witches set their own rules regarding appropriate undergarments.

The gone-astray garb beneath Opal's dress, however, was just the beginning of her appalling fashion blunders.

Showy jewelry was a rarity in our neighborhood. Yet thick rings glittering with gaudy, colored glass adorned each of Opal's fingers.

"Those dime store rings make her look cheap and vulgar," Mom often criticized.

Conventional-minded mothers on Jennings Road agreed that a woman shouldn't appear in public with her hair untamed, or, worse yet, dyed. So whenever Opal changed the tint of her hair—and she experimented with garish colors often—a barrage of shameful and outrageous accusations spewed forth from the mouths of mothers who were ditch-water blondes or mundane brunettes.

Despite their disapproval of our neighbor's mode of dressing and poor taste, I still wished for a mother as tousled and exotic as Opal. Despite fearing her evil eye, I wished that she would look my way. So when the ragtag child at the rear of the parade passed by, I stuck my head through a gap in the lilies.

"Hey, little girl. You going to the store?"

The child's hair stuck out in one-inch spikes all over her scalp. The heads of her brothers were shaved to the skin.

"It's a dead giveaway the whole tribe is infested with lice," Mom had asserted the previous day.

The poky-haired girl turned her bug-ridden head away from me and continued walking.

I often had watched with envy as Opal's scruffy brood squatted on the cracked linoleum at Midland Gardens Mercantile picking out their penny candies. Would they opt for red-hot balls of bubble gum, candy cigarettes with glowing, pink tips, malted milk balls, tiny wax bottles filled with sticky juice, black licorice twists, or

242

pastel packets of tangy Smarties? The children's grubby hands fingered the unwrapped candies as they pondered their choices. In the end, they got one of each.

"Opal spends all their Welfare money on candy," Diana told me as we crouched behind the lilies.

"It's a waste of the taxpayer's money," I added, sounding very much like my mother.

But I still wished that my much-maligned neighbor would buy *me* a piece of candy. The indulgent woman doled out fistfuls of dimes to her children—their snotty-nosed, radiant faces upturned to hers. Because my folks saved their hard-earned nickels for a rainy day, I longed for parents who were wanton and wasteful like Opal. I wished that my family could go on Welfare so Mom and Dad might give me a dime every day.

"If we had something to sell, we could buy our own candy," I said as the motley crew passed from sight.

"I'd buy roller skates," Diana said.

We both held hopes of becoming contenders on the televised Roller Derby.

So, enlivened by the challenge of earning my own money to buy skates, I commenced to cogitate. A simple plan shortly surfaced.

"We could sell Holy Water," I suggested.

My friend Linda, a Catholic, had told me of its mystical, protective powers.

Holy Water! Because Diana wasn't inclined to give me credit, I patted myself on the back for conjuring up the resourceful scheme. *By the end of the day, we'll both be rich!*

So Diana and I trudged through the ditches on both sides of Jennings Road, poking through moldering leaves and putrefying grass in search of empty beer bottles. We packed a cardboard box until it overflowed, and then filled the brown bottles with algae-green water from the pond in The Nether Woods.

Diana cleaned her hands on the front of her pedal pushers while I packed the bottles into the box. Our tennis shoes squished as we walked the muddy path that circled the pond. Diana led the way. I lugged the box.

We peddled the Holy Water from door to door for ten cents a bottle or two for a quarter. Even though few of the housewives on Jennings Road were Catholics, nearly all of them bought one. Three of our neighbors agreed to buy two—but not before quibbling about the quarter and questioning our arithmetic skills.

Opal's house at the bottom of the hill was the last stop on our route. The ramshackle dwelling sank deeper into the soggy ground each day. Shielded by the Holy Water, we ascended the crumbling cement steps, and then hesitantly banged the knocker. The little poky-haired girl swung the door wide-open.

I had given much consideration as to how the house of a witch should be furnished, so I anticipated a room hazy with the smoke of incense and heavy with glitz. A scrawny, black cat would turn her head toward me, and then sharpen her claws on the back of a red velvet couch. I had imagined yellowed candles sputtering on a shelf, their flickering flames creating wavy shadows that danced across the tattered tapestries hanging limply from the walls.

But the interior of Opal's home, although more kid-worn than my own, looked like any other house on Jennings Road.

"Go fetch your momma's purse, honey," Diana sweetly ordered. "You can buy these bottles of Holy Water all by yourself." She displayed the remaining bottles before her. "If you drink a little every morning, you'll never get spanked again."

Because I could benefit from the same protection, I made a wish that we would lose the sale. But alas, the girl took the bottles, and then scuttled off to retrieve the purse.

Diana's eyes grew as round as penny gumballs when Opal's daughter returned with a ten dollar bill. She snatched the money, grabbed my hand, hopped the porch, and dashed down the driveway—all the while urging me to run faster. There was no need to hurry me along, however. I was pumping my legs for all they were worth.

"You didn't give that girl her change," I said when we reached Diana's porch.

The afternoon air was oppressively still, yet wind chimes tinkled ominously from the eaves above us. Eyes fixed on the crest of the hill, Diana's hand slowly turned the doorknob.

"That was probably Opal's grocery money for the next two weeks," I said. "You better give it back."

Diana opened the door wide enough to squeeze through, slipped inside, and then banged it closed behind her.

So much for Opal getting back her money, I thought.

I glanced toward the hill. Not a single neighbor was about, yet I felt the dark eyes of Opal upon me. To make myself scarce, I hid in the salmonberry thicket in the woods behind my backyard until I heard Momma call me to dinner.

After a three day, self-imposed exile, Diana emerged from her house. Secured around her neck with a sky-blue ribbon, a silver skate key glinted in the luminous sun. She pulled it over her head and twirled it on her finger as she clattered by my house on shiny, new skates. Tumbling over potholes and loose gravel, she rattled up and down the road. On account of her lack of grace, both knees and elbows soon were bloodied.

I fumed on my front porch as she paraded before me. There would be no candy, no cookies, and no frozen TV dinners—not so much as a crumb to feed Opal's urchins for the next two weeks. I felt sorry for the little girl, but I felt sorrier for myself. Not only had Diana spent Opal's ten dollars, she'd kept my share of the dimes besides.

Yet wasn't it I who had been pocketing a rabbit's foot, searching for four-leaf clovers, and scanning the sky for falling stars every night? My fervent and ongoing wish had never once wavered—to become the owner of a pair of skates so I could commence my training for the Roller Derby. Unless I could think of something else to sell, I would never join the ranks of those gutsy women.

The following morning, Diana eyed the shoes heaped on our back porch while tapping her sneakered foot. "Somebody swiped my skates," she said.

Apparently, I was her primary suspect.

Because we had fleeced Opal of a ten-dollar bill, police cars, jail cells, starving children, evil eyes, broken bottles of Holy Water, and counterfeit ten dollar bills had dominated my dreams four nights in a row. Diana, however, showed no sign of remorse as she paced the patio.

Suddenly, Opal crested the hill. We sought shelter indoors as the penniless woman and her hungry kids trooped past my house. Keeping low to the sill, we watched them through the living room window.

The poky-haired girl was last in the line of seven children. Secured around her neck with a soiled blue ribbon, Diana's silver skate key glinted in the luminous sun. Shod in her rightful plunder, the girl glided before my house on silver skates. She skirted potholes and loose gravel with inherent skill and grace. Weaving in and out between her brothers, she twirled in circles and made perfect figure-eights. The brazen bandit flaunted her booty with shameless guile.

Diana's face paled. Her freckles stood out like a sickly pox. For a certainty, fury would consume my neighbor in the days to follow, but I doubted that she'd work up the courage to reclaim those sullied skates. Nor would she become the national Roller Derby skating champion—a dream that she'd aspired to since moving next door.

From the way the little poky-haired girl had taken to those skates, it was *she* who would claim that title. I meant to befriend the wily thief and skip along beside her as she skated down The Road to Glory.

We'd fuel up along the way, of course, with pocketsful of penny candy.

Twins

I never had a twin sister, but I wished for one all the same. I searched for her too in a crowd. With lopsided pigtails and canted bangs just like mine, I would recognize my twin right away.

∿ ๑

My twin, if I'd had one, was born with a vague Something Wrong, and nobody talked about it. Four legs and twelve fingers? One brown eye, one blue? A backwards, sideways, or upside-down head? Perhaps she had no head at all! Two belly buttons? Pointed ears? A missing arm? No hair? No toes?

No matter.

My mom, I imagined, had given her away to the gypsies, to a sailor, or to a roving bluegrass band. Yet through many years and even more miles, my twin never forgot me—her sister. Wherever she roamed, my twin sought me out. She searched for a path that would lead her to me.

So I would wait for a million years—and a hundred more after that.

I would wait until the Kingdom came—even if it never showed up.

I would wait until our shadows matched up.

I would wait until our dreams collided.
And then...
My twin would smile.
Our fingers would touch.
And I would be whole at last.

∽ ∾

Together we'd build a hut in the forest.
No one would look for us there.

World Travelers

The black jalopy rested on flat tires in a lean-to behind our garage. Its windshield was cracked. The wipers lacked blades. The turn signals didn't turn on. Rubber bands, paper clips, and two miles of friction tape held its engine parts in place. The missing carburetor, spark plugs, alternator, and battery had been replaced with soup cans, clothespins, and cracker boxes.

Renovation of the vintage car had been a neighborhood venture. It entailed five days of enthusiastic labor and occupied ten children from three different families. But in spite of our earnest efforts, that rusted-out rattletrap would never roll again. We didn't care. Red and yellow flames, hand-painted by a pint-sized pit crew, blazed along its sides.

The car's back seat was missing, but four of us could bounce comfortably on the cracked leather seat in front. We took turns driving. As we stretched stubbed toes to the limit, our feet strained to reach the pedals. We ran through the gears with practiced ease. Although speeds upwards of five hundred miles per hour were exceeded, the driver seldom put a foot to the brakes.

Mrs. Ross, the divorcee living in the rental next door, reclined on a fold-up chaise lounge on her side of a much-climbed-over wire fence. She supervised our projects and mediated our frequent squabbles.

Mrs. Ross' freckled shoulders were shiny with Johnson's Baby Oil. Her bright red hair was a glorious sight. She wore a blouse with a ruffled bodice that enhanced her chest, and matching pink shorts that were outrageously high on her thigh. A dozen silver bangle bracelets jingled on her wrist as she hollered out destinations plucked from a fat world atlas—its spine broken in three places.

"Take a left at Morocco."

"It's just around the corner from Zanzibar."

"Only another five hundred miles."

"Step on the gas!"

Our neighbor peeked at us over Hollywood sunglasses studded with genuine rhinestones as we traversed scorching deserts, ferried across stormy seas, roared over winding mountain passes, and arrived at our chosen destination with a thud and a grinding of gears. The jalopy was out of gas, had a dead battery, and the radiator was boiling over. A pit crew of aspiring mechanics moved in with rusty wrenches, bent screwdrivers, and a coffee can filled with odd lengths of electrical wire, rolls of friction tape, and an assortment of nuts and bolts. While an attendant refueled the vehicle with water from the garden hose, others banged and poked at the engine with pliers and hammers. Someone pumped at the flat tires. Within five minutes, a fresh driver and three new passengers embarked on another adventure. Each unique journey was mapped out and navigated by Mrs. Ross, our travel agent.

"It's just across the Bering Strait."

"Head north at the Gulf of Guinea."

"Now shift down to third, and for heaven's sake, slow down, sweetie, or you'll miss the Ural Mountains!"

Our classmates would return to school in the fall boasting of trips to Disneyland, but our neighborhood gang would not be impressed. Our parents lacked the funds for extravagant excursions, but we didn't care. We couldn't wait to brag about our own vacations.

"The headhunters of Borneo stretch their earlobes six inches or more with iron rings. They settle their arguments by seeing who can stay underwater the longest."

"The worst drivers in Europe are Belgians. Even the French say so. Nobody drives a convertible there. It rains three hundred days of the year."

"The main attraction of Romania is Dracula's Castle. People there believe that a mud-bath is good for your health."

Our classmates' jaws would hang wide open as we fabricated tales about our exotic adventures. Not one of them would dare to dispute us, and incredulous teachers would hold their tongues.

We knew our geography, after all, for we had traveled the world.

Summer's End

Picking around the edges of a scab.
Watching an anthill.
Looking for four-leaf clovers.
Counting stars.
Finding shapes in the clouds.
Catching grasshoppers.
Tying chains of clover.
Digging for the devil.
Chasing the ice cream wagon with nary a penny in our pockets...

So many activities!

So much sunshine!

So many ways to waste our time!

None of us had anything to show for our day, but not a child amongst us cared.

Each summer had passed like the one before.

The next summer would be just the same.

∽ ∽

And so I wish I had a photo of the eight of us poised on the stream bank—Fred, Ted, Evie, Judy, Markie, Kenny, Little Kathy, and me.

Mud up to our elbows.

Mud splattering and freckling our cheeks.

261

Mud between our toes.

We dammed up the stream with boulders and branches. We poked clods of dirt and muddy sod into the gaps. The leaks were stopped up with moldered leaves.

Laughing.

Splashing.

Joking.

Shoving.

We collapsed on the bank—bare, brown legs dangling in the pool we had formed, arms flopped behind our heads, eyes searching for blue skies through the shimmering leaves above.

It never occurred to any of us that summer would end.

It never occurred to any of us that we would grow up.

Acknowledgments

The friends and family members who enriched my childhood deserve my wholehearted thanks. They shared with me varied—and sometimes conflicting—memories, details, and facts about the summer of 1962 and inspired me to record them.

I also thank my husband Kurt for encouraging me to follow through with my project, my friend Darrell White for his proofreading and enthusiasm, and The Wenatchee Valley Writers for helping me hone my craft.

My grandson Gunnar, featured on the cover, carries on the legacy of the Cleveland belly button.

Belly Button Blues is Teresa Wendel's first published collection of personal essays. Her short stories and essays have been featured in national, regional, and local magazines and newspapers. Teresa lives in Wenatchee, Washington with her husband Kurt.

Made in the USA
Charleston, SC
21 March 2012